Andrew Foldi
Courtesy of Santa Fe Opera
Ken Howard, Photographer

ACKNOWLEDGEMENTS

I wish to express my profound thanks to my stepson, Gregory R. Hancock, for his interest, time and devotion in creating the caricatures for this book and to Michel Singher and H. David Kaplan for their dedication and painstaking effort in assisting with proofreading the text.

The caricature of me on the front cover was made by the late Franco Calabrese, at the time of our appearance in *LULU* in Florence, Italy in 1985.

OPERA:
AN ACCIDENT
WAITING TO HAPPEN
(40 Years of Musical Mishaps)

by Andrew Foldi

LEYERLE
PUBLICATIONS

OPERA: AN ACCIDENT WAITING TO HAPPEN
by
Andrew Foldi

Copyright © 1999 Leyerle Publications

ISBN 1-878617-28-1

LEYERLE PUBLICATIONS
Executive Offices
28 Stanley Street
Mt. Morris, New York 14510

This book can be ordered directly from

LEYERLE
PUBLICATIONS
Box 384
Geneseo, New York 14454

CONTENTS

I dedicate this book to my wife, Marta for her love, patience and understanding, to my children Nancy and David, and their mother, Leona, who managed to survive the early years and to Marta's sons, Greg and Chris, who also go into this mess periodically.

INTRODUCTION

I think it says everything about Andrew Foldi, the performer, that he received an excellent notice in the New York Daily News for a performance he did *NOT* give of "Dansker" in BILLY BUDD at the Metropolitan Opera on April 5, 1989 — no, it was not that the reviewer was mistaken about who sang that night. It was that the reviewer had seen Andrew Foldi do the role in a previous season and could not help missing him in the current run. That's how Andy's performances were — whatever character he played became, for the audience, indelible. Whether it was Dansker, or Dr. Bartolo, or Baron Ochs, or Schigolch; whatever the language, whatever the style, whether the character was good or evil, funny or tragic, once you saw Andy Foldi play it, you had a hard time accepting anyone else.

However, I have been privileged to know Andy not only as a performer, but also as a teacher, administrator, coach, stage director and friend, and he is as distinctive and irreplaceable in all these capacities as he is on stage. I have enjoyed many dinners with him and his lovely wife Marta, and the stories you are about to read have kept us laughing long into the night. For those of you who don't yet know Andy Foldi, you are in for a treat.

Lenore Rosenberg
Associate Artistic Administrator
Metropolitan Opera

ANDREW FOLDI
BIOGRAPHY

Born in Budapest and raised in the United States, Metropolitan Opera bass-baritone Andrew Foldi has been recognized as one of the finest basso-buffos in the United States and Europe. During his career Mr. Foldi has sung with virtually every major opera company on both continents.

In 1981, while still singing, he was appointed Chairman of the Opera Department of the Cleveland Institute of Music. In 1991 he became the Director of the Lyric Opera Center for American Artists in Chicago, retiring in 1995.

He started to study piano at age five in Budapest, ultimately entering the University of Chicago as a musicology major in 1943. While still a student, he became music critic of the *Chicago Times* in 1947. After his stint as critic, he began serious vocal studies with Richard deYoung and the noted French baritone Martial Singher.

He was one of the three initial audition winners of the then newly-formed Lyric Theater of Chicago in 1954, joining the Santa Fe Opera in its initial season in 1957, the San Francisco Opera in 1960 and became the leading basso-buffo of the opera in Zurich in 1961. While living in Europe he sang at La Scala in Milan, the Staatsoper in Vienna and many other opera companies and festivals. He moved back to the United States in 1974 when he joined the Metropolitan Opera, where he sang until 1988. He has an operatic repertoire of more than one hundred roles. He has an extensive concert repertoire and has appeared with James Levine at the Met and at the Ravinia Festival, with Seiji Ozawa both in Boston and in San Francisco, with Bernard Haitink at the Concertgebouw in Amsterdam, with Rafael Kubelik with the New York Philharmonic, the Chicago Symphony Orchestra and the Bayerischer Rundfunk in Munich, with Christoph von Dohnányi and the Cleveland Orchestra at Severance Hall and at Carnegie Hall and at the Blossom Festival. He has directed around thirty operas, both professionally as well as at the Cleveland Institute and Chicago's Lyric Opera Center.

Mr. Foldi has been associated with many eminent composers, such as Paul Hindemith, Zoltán Kodály, Benjamin Britten, Ernest Bloch, Gian Carlo Menotti, Ernst Toch, Carlisle Floyd and Igor Stravinsky. He appeared with Mr. Stravinsky on several occasions and was invited by the composer to sing the American premiere of his ABRAHAM AND ISAAC.

Mr. Foldi returned to the Metropolitan Opera for the last time in the spring of 1988 for his seventeenth production of Alban Berg's LULU, to repeat his world-famous characterization of Schigolch, which was seen on television during the 1980-81 season in *Live from the Met*. He has sung this role more than 100 times in three languages, including the American premiere of the three-act version in Santa Fe in English, the Ljubimov production in Chicago in the autumn of 1987 and in Torino in 1983 in German, at the Maggio Musicale in Florence in the spring of 1985 in Italian and at numerous other opera houses, including those of San Francisco, Geneva, and Amsterdam. He has sung every performance of the opera at the Met since its Metropolitan premiere in 1977.

Andrew Porter in *The New Yorker* has called his Schigolch a "virtuoso performance," Paul Hume in *The Washington Post* "unforgettable," Harold Schonberg in *The New York Times* "brilliant," and the late Robert Jacobson in *Opera News* "a classic" and "the definitive Schigolch." Mr. Foldi's analysis of the character has been published both by *Opera News* and the *Newsletter of the Alban Berg Society*.

Mr. Foldi has sung a wide variety of roles at the Met, including Beckmesser in DIE MEISTERSINGER, Alberich in the RING, the Sacristan in TOSCA, Le Bailli in WERTHER, as well as the two Bartolos in LE NOZZE DI FIGARO and IL BARBIERE DI SIVIGLIA. In the latter role he also received unanimous critical acclaim from the British press at the Glyndebourne Festival and the Spanish press in Barcelona. He has sung the Rossini Bartolo more than 300 times in three languages and made a recording of the opera for Concert Hall Records and a film in German for Austrian Television.

His other Rossini recordings include Don Magnifico and Mustafa for Concert Hall and Macrobio in *LA PIETRA DEL PARAGONE* for Vanguard which was reissued on CD. His recording of Tevye in *FIDDLER ON THE ROOF* was also released by Concert Hall. His oratorio recordings include the title role of Handel's *SAUL* (La Voix d'Église and Alcanta), Schönberg's *A MODERN PSALM* (Columbia), Daniel and Gobrias in Handel's *BELSHAZZAR*, Beethoven's *RUINS OF ATHENS* and *CANTATA ON THE DEATH OF JOSEPH II* (Concert Hall).

Mr. Foldi's television appearances, in addition to Schigolch and Bartolo, include his portrayal of Baron Zeta in *THE MERRY WIDOW* with Beverly Sills and Dulcamara in the production of *THE ELIXIR OF LOVE* conceived by James deBlasis, which was filmed in 1978 for PBS.

PRELUDE

Over the years it happened often enough that colleagues, students, or friends at parties, would ask if anything ever happened to me on stage that was amusing or unusual. After a career of forty plus-years, enough incidents have occured to regale them with an assortment of stories. I will narrate some that I hope the reader might find entertaining.

IGOR STRAVINSKY

I shall start in 1959 for no special reason other than to bring Igor Stravinsky's name to this collection with an unforgettable event singing under his baton.

When the Santa Fe Opera was founded by John Crosby in 1957, one of his ingenious ideas was to bring the great composer out to New Mexico, thereby giving the Festival instant recognition and prestige. For those of us singing with the company in those years, it was a truly exciting experience to watch the great man at work and, depending on the repertoire of the season, to have a chance to work with him.

IGOR STRAVINSKY'S *THRENI*

A gala concert was planned for the summer of 1959 in the St. Francis Cathedral, culminating in a performance of Stravinsky's oratorio *THRENI*, based on the Lamentations of Jeremiah. The work, written shortly after Stravinsky embraced serialism[1] in his compositions, is one of great complexity and difficulty, putting the performers, instrumentalists, chorus and soloists on their mettle to master the musical difficulties of performing the oratorio. It has a section of unaccompanied canons[2] for the four male voices (2

1 See *Serialism* in Glossary.
2 See *Canon* in Glossary.

tenors, baritone and bass) based on a twelve-tone row[1] and its various combinations and permutations. As rehearsals progressed, it became evident that of the four male soloists, the baritone was having a great deal of difficulty finding his pitches. Mr. Stravinsky, knowing that I had perfect pitch, arranged the way we were to stand at the concert so that the baritone and I, the bass, should be on his right and the two tenors on his left. To be on the safe side, he asked that whenever the baritone was the first to begin one of these canons, I should hum his note for him. He was to hum the note quietly back to me and I was to nod to Mr. Stravinsky that all was well. All this, of course, was to take merely seconds.

At the concert not only did we have the usual pre-concert tensions, but our baritone was exceptionally nervous. He was to start the second canon and before I had a chance to hum his note as was pre-arranged, he already began to sing — a half step flat and before Mr. Stravinsky gave the downbeat. I was the second one to sing in the canon and made an instant decision to go with the baritone and his error, which meant having to transpose[2] twelve-tone rows during the concert — a rather nerve-wracking experience. I figured at least we would be together and the audience surely would not be the wiser for it. But as Mr. Stravinsky did not skip with us and began his beat only on the baritone's second note, we were one beat ahead of him. The first tenor, on Mr. Stravinsky's left on the other side of the cathedral, either didn't hear us or decided to try to correct matters. He came in correctly, which meant that he was a beat behind us, and even worse, singing a half step higher than the two of us. The second tenor, by now totally confused, came in singing something or other, and as he began, Mr. Stravinsky stopped conducting, folded his hands, looked upwards and smiled.

1See *Serialism* in Glossary.
2 See *Transposition* in Glossary.

We finished the chaotic canon somehow and when the next section was to begin, Mr. Stravinsky once again began to conduct. We managed the rest of the oratorio without any more major disasters. There was a reception following the concert at the La Fonda hotel, where the four of us rushed up to Mr. Stravinsky, who was comfortably seated by then enjoying his scotch, to ask him "Maestro, why did you stop conducting?" "My dear children," he responded in his high-pitched voice, "you were so lost that only God could help. So I prayed."

THRENI proved to be an interesting part of my repertoire throughout my career and I used a portion of the piece, an unaccompanied monodia[1] for the bass at almost all my auditions. Even though it is not from an opera and the monodia is but a minute and a half in duration, I assumed that it would be something that would catch the attention of anyone who was auditioning me. The sustained legato singing, in addition to giving me an opportunity to show off my voice, especially the low register, would surely arouse the curiosity of the person listening because it does show something about one's musical talent that other selections might not easily reveal.

1See *Monodia* in Glossary.

BEGINNING A SINGING CAREER

My professional operatic career began in Chicago when I was one of the three winners of the new Lyric Theater's audition in 1954. The next major step was appearing with the Santa Fe Opera at ITS birth in 1957, and in many subsequent seasons. In the fall of 1961, I moved to Switzerland with my family, where I started my European career, by accepting the invitation of Dr. Herbert Graf to become the leading basso buffo of the Zurich Opera, subsequently moving to Geneva when he also changed his base of operations to that city.

In the spring of 1962 my agent called me with an offer to replace an ailing Leporello in a performance of Mozart's *DON GIOVANNI* at the Amsterdam Opera. I arrived the night before the performance. The next morning I had a one-hour run-through of some recitatives with the stage director and the artist singing the title role — the Italian baritone Scipio Colombo. In the evening at the performance, I was already in my dressing room warming up when there was a knock on the door. The conductor came in to introduce himself and ask me if I had any special wishes. It is not unusual in such emergencies, especially in European repertory houses, that when a singer "jumps into" a role he/she knows, that there is a minimum of rehearsal and that one only meets the rest of one's colleagues during the performance on stage. It saves the theater from having to shut down the house that night, but artistically it can leave a lot to be desired. The conductor and I had only enough time to talk through the tempo of the Catalogue Aria and I went to the stage just in time to hear the overture since I had to be there immediately as the curtain rose. It became clear as I listened to the overture that this conductor was simply fabulous, even though this was his very first opera. That was my introduction to Bernard Haitink.

AUDITIONS

This leads into my next topic, which is surely the most feared and hated experience of any performer, auditions. Auditions take place in weird settings, often under adverse conditions. Often the room is an acoustical nightmare, the piano may be out of tune, the pianist may not be exactly great, or even if the pianist is good, the two artists may be on different musical wavelengths.

Over the years I sang many auditions for conductors, opera directors, managers — whoever would listen — and I wound up going back to Amsterdam to sing an audition for the Concertgebouw Orchestra. Although by then Bernard Haitink was the chief conductor of the orchestra, I had to audition for the general director of the orchestra, the composer Marius Flothuis.

As was my habit, I began with the *THRENI* monodia and after I sang it, Mr. Flothuis asked how I knew that they were going to perform this next year, as it was a deeply guarded secret. He was quite amused by the fact that I had no idea about it and that I just used the monodia to begin all my auditions. Happily, he was pleased by what he heard, and the orchestra hired me for that concert on the spot.

In addition to the oratorio being performed in the regular concert series, it was also performed in a Sunday afternoon modern music series, in which it was Mr. Haitink's custom to play one of the works twice in the concert: once before intermission and once afterwards. I thought it a marvellous idea, as works of this nature cannot really be grasped on first hearing and this way the audience would have a chance to hear it twice right then and there. It was fascinating to watch the faces in the audience the second time around as the work was now more familiar and began to make wonderful musical sense to some of the listeners, who were modern-music aficionados in the first place.

For many years I tried various ways to get an audition for Leonard Bernstein, but in spite of the wonderful help of my late colleague and close friend, Judith Raskin, there seemed to be no way to get to sing for him. However, my agent did succeed in getting me an audition for Lorin Maazel, at that time the musical director of the Berlin Opera. This was arranged to take place after one of his rehearsals at Avery Fisher Hall in New York. Auditions by their very nature are nerve-wracking, and singing on the stage of Avery Fisher Hall for a conductor as demanding as Lorin Maazel made me especially nervous.

I was given a room to warm up in and began, after a few scales and exercises, to sing the *THRENI* monodia, with which I intended to begin the audition again. There was a knock on the door and to my response of "Come in," a gentleman from next door stuck his face into the room. It was Leonard Bernstein. He was intrigued to hear the Stravinsky being sung — hardly your normal audition aria — and wanted to know what I was doing here. When I explained that I am singing an audition for Mr. Maazel, he asked me if I thought Mr. Maazel would mind if he would also come down and listen to my audition. As I explained that I have no idea if Mr. Maazel will mind, I was jumping for joy as suddenly this audition was to be for two great conductors and the audition for Leonard Bernstein that I was never able to get, was materializing on the spur of the moment before my eyes.

When it was time, I went down to the stage, Mr. Berstein came in, sat next to Mr. Maazel, explained his presence to him and my audition began. After the *THRENI* monodia both yelled bravo and I proceeded to sing an audition that lasted well over half an hour, singing a wide variety of repertoire, ranging from Leporello's Catalogue Aria from *DON GIOVANNI*, Baron Ochs's monologue from the end of the second act of

DER ROSENKAVALIER, and Alberich's curse from *DAS RHEINGOLD* to Dr. Bartolo's aria from *THE BARBER OF SEVILLE*. Each aria was greeted with enthusiastic bravos and applause (no one EVER applauds at an audition) and I saw in front of me the making of my career. How wrong I was!

After it was all over Mr. Bernstein left and Mr. Maazel came up to talk to me. He was simply furious that Bernstein was there. No matter how I tried to explain the weird succession of events, he insisted that I had it all arranged and left in a huff. After all the enthusiasm from BOTH of them, neither one ever hired me. It was a bitter lesson to find out just how little some responses mean at auditions and indeed never to count on any engagement, let alone a career, until one gets it in writing.

When my family and I were on vacation on the West Coast following the Santa Fe season of 1958, upon our arrival in San Francisco I called Kurt Herbert Adler, whom I had met previously in Chicago, to inquire if he might be able to hear me in an audition for the San Francisco Opera. As opposed to the audition for Lorin Maazel and Leonard Bernstein described above, this was a very brief one. I sang a couple of arias, exceptionally badly I might add, got no response whatsoever from Mr. Adler other than a perfunctory "thank you" afterwards and chalked it up to a bad experience. I was utterly dumbfounded when the phone rang at the hotel the next morning and Mr. Adler, calling personally, offered me a contract for the following season singing a vast assortment of secondary roles with the company.

Since my chances for advancement in Chicago after six seasons of comprimario roles were obviously nil, I gladly accepted the offer. Somewhere there is a curious moral to all this — sing a good audition and be offered nothing; sing a terrible audition and be offered a nice contract. So much for self-evaluation.

One of the more curious auditions that I sang one year was for Peter Herman Adler and the NBC Television Opera. This was arranged by George Schick who was the Assistant Conductor of the Chicago Symphony Orchestra during Rafael Kubelik's regime and who took a liking to my work as a result of two concerts I was engaged to sing with Mr. Kubelik.

This was before my *THRENI* days, so I began with Verdi's "Il lacerato spirito" from *SIMON BOCCANEGRA*, an aria that an old friend, the bass Ken Smith, dubbed the national anthem of basses. The aria doesn't go very high, thus it can be a "safe" aria for starters. It shows legato singing, it shows the low register without necessarily plumbing into the lowest depths and, when all is said and done, is an aria that helps to warm up the voice. I had barely sung a little bit of the aria when I noticed Mr. Adler shaking his head in a negative manner. Unnerving as this was, he did ask for another selection, continuing with his apparent disapproval all during the second aria as well. When he came up to talk to me afterwards I finally realized that his "negations" were really a nervous "tic" he was not able to control. Although I was relieved it was not a disapproval, I was sorry he had the affliction.

In the early sixties, after our move to Zurich, I sang an unsuccessful audition for Glyndebourne. The pianist for the audition was Viola Tunnard, who also was working at the time with Benjamin Britten. She thought that he should hear me and arranged that I sing an audition for him in December of 1964, on my way back from San Francisco to Zurich. As it worked out, I was to have an audition directly before I was to catch my flight from London to The Hague, where I was to meet with a manager before getting home.

I had my customary load of many months' travel: suitcase, tape recorder over a shoulder, a carry-on bag that seemed to weigh a ton by then, and hat and coat for any weather eventuality. I piled all this into a taxi which wended its way out to Mr. Britten's residence, which seemed to be located "behind God's back," as we used to say in Hungary about far-away locations.

I rang the bell and as I looked up to the second or third floor after entering the building, I saw Peter Pears peering down in utter incredulity at this bizarre apparition below with all the luggage. Mr. Pears was Mr. Britten's long-time companion, and it was for him that all of Britten's tenor roles were written. "Are YOU Mr. Foldi?" After my assenting response he said, "Well, do come up" in a voice that was clearly a sound of disbelief watching this mountain of junk below.

As I had assumed this would hardly be the "usual" operatic audition, I had prepared an assortment of pieces in various styles and from various historical periods. I began with the inevitable a cappella *THRENI* excerpt, which certainly roused both their curiosities.

After looking through my collection, Mr. Britten chose a sacred concerto of Viadana for solo bass, a composition I sang at some of my recitals. An amusing dialogue occurred. "Peter, do play for him. I would like to sit back and listen." "No, Benjy, I would prefer if you would play." "No, I insist." This went on for a while until Peter Pears finally sat down at the piano while Benjamin Britten sat on the couch and I sang the composition. After that, further inquiries as to what I had with me. Finally, a question from Britten: "Do you have any songs of Kodály, perchance?" "No," I responded, "but I do have two song cycles of Bartók with me." They were "Village Scenes" and "Eight Hungarian folksongs." Mr. Britten chose the first two songs of the former cycle and then the same conversation about who was to play for me resumed. Mr. Pears sat down at the piano as I presented him with the music— the song cycle copied out in my own handwriting as I had to transpose it for my voice range. The printed version only existed in the original high key. Peter Pears took one look at it and said, "I can't possibly read this miserable hen-scratching," referring to my wretched calligraphy. Britten walked over and he also was horrified and asked me who could have possibly done such a terrible job of copying. I confessed that I was the culprit, at which point another few minutes of discussion continued between them as to who should play. I was getting very "antsy" at this point because I was afraid that I would miss my flight if this went on much longer. I piped up with my suggestion that if they didn't mind, since I have a plane to catch very soon, I would play for myself — as I knew the songs, after all — and they could both listen. They jumped at this suggestion, and there I was playing the piano with Britten and Pears, two consummate pianists, listening. Although as a child I was passable as a pianist, by now my finger skills had deteriorated badly from lack of any regular practice. Both gentlemen were very pleasant and complimentary (about the singing, I hasten to add, not about my pianism) and we bade each other adieu as they called a taxi for me and I headed out to Heathrow.

A few months later I received a letter from Benjamin Britten inviting me to the Aldeburgh Festival to sing some of Kodály's songs at a concert they had planned in his honor as well as offering me the part of the Abbot in the world premiere of his new opera, *CURLEW RIVER*. Needless to say, I was very pleased by this turn of events.

Not many weeks later a second letter arrived. Mr. Britten indicated that there was no problem with the Kodály concert but that the Home Office would not grant me a labor permit for *CURLEW RIVER* unless he could swear under oath that there was no bass in the British Empire who could sing the part. Obviously, that was hardly the case and he asked me to release him from the previous offer for the part of the Abbot. Under the circumstances, of course, I did so unhesitatingly. There was still the Kodály concert, which indeed did take place the following summer with the composer in attendance.

THE LYRIC OPERA OF CHICAGO

I will now backtrack many years to 1954. My career really started seriously when I was one of the three audition winners of the newly-formed Lyric Opera, or as it was called then, Lyric Theater. My assignments for that first season were my debut as Biondello in Vittorio Giannini's *THE TAMING OF THE SHREW*, Dr. Grenvil in *LA TRAVIATA* with Callas, Simoneau and Gobbi, and Sciarrone in *TOSCA* with Steber, DiStefano and Gobbi. All were conducted by the company's music director, Nicola Rescigno. I decided that I would learn every bass part in the repertory as I figured you never know when that might come in handy.

On the day of the dress rehearsal of *CARMEN* I was at home when the phone rang. It was Carol Fox, founder and general director of Lyric Theater, on the line. She wanted to know if I knew the role of Zuniga, because the singer assigned to the role was shaky musically. When I told her that I knew it cold, she told me to come down to the opera house immediately.

Upon my arrival, I found out that I would sing the dress rehearsal, not having done a single rehearsal myself, although, fortunately, I had watched some rehearsals in the house. The cast included Giulietta Simionato in the title role and the baritone, Giangiacomo Guelfi, as Escamillo. Jonel Perlea, the conductor, and William Wymetal, the stage director, seemed to have been pleased, as I was given both performances after that dress rehearsal.

It turned out that was not all I wound up doing at these performances. The company's music staff in those years was very small, and there were no assistant conductors to spare to attend to an unexpected task in the third act. It seems that Mr. Guelfi had trouble hearing the orchestra from backstage when he sang part of the Toreador Song at the end of the act and I was asked to play the harmonium for him so he could get his notes.

The following season, once again, I decided to learn all the bass parts and I was called down one day to a rehearsal of *I PURITANI* to sing some of the cues of Giorgio for a chorus rehearsal. Nicola Rossi-Lemeni, who was singing the role had not yet arrived in town from Italy.

On the day of the dress rehearsal the phone rang. I rushed to answer it, hoping that once again I was being called to sing, only this time a major role. (The "rest" of that cast was Callas, DiStefano and Bastianini, no less). It was Larry Kelly, the co-director of the company calling. This time, it seems, they had run out of assistant conductors again. There was no one left to do light cues and they needed someone who could read music for this task. "Would you be willing to do it?" I explained to him that I had never done light cues in my life, but if they were willing, I was certainly willing to give it a try.

I hopped into my car and rushed downtown to the opera house, where I was quickly ushered to meet Jean Rosenthal, the renowned lighting designer. She gave me a crash course in doing light cues which, in fact, is not all that difficult. Each cue has a number. At X measures before the lighting change is to be affected, one says, "Warning for Cue whatever number" over a microphone to the person controlling the light board. Then at the appointed moment one says, "Go, Cue whatever number" and that's that.

My only concern was that in the heat of the excitement and trying to see and hear the opera with THAT cast being a serious distraction from the task at hand, I would unwittingly plunge Madame Callas, or whomever, into total darkness by mistake. Fortunately, all went smoothly. I still have my score from that occasion and it is amazing to realize that there were but a total of 29 light cues! Today there would be many hundreds, not to mention computerized lightboards and sophisticated lighting equipment.

After that season, the management of the company split up. Messrs. Kelly and Rescigno went to Dallas to found that company (taking Callas with them) and Carol Fox remained in Chicago to run the Lyric by herself. As a result of a successful re-audition for her, I was given some better parts in 1956. These included Masetto in *DON GIOVANNI* and the First Nazarene in *SALOME*. Both of these were to be conducted by a man from Frankfurt, new to these shores, Georg Solti. One does get to meet a very interesting collection of people in an opera company of such renown and I became quite friendly with Paul Schöffler, who was singing the Commendatore in *DON GIOVANNI*. He himself was a former Giovanni in his younger days. He was also assigned to sing Wotan in *DIE WALKÜRE* (which was also conducted by Georg Solti).

I went to all the performances I could in those days and was especially anxious to hear the *WALKÜRE*, because Schöffler rarely sang Wotan. He felt the role was too dramatic for his voice, unlike Hans Sachs in *DIE MEISTERSINGER*, which was a role he "owned." We sat in the artists' box for the performance, which began a little like the Marx Brothers' *A NIGHT AT THE OPERA*. Early in the first act one of the string players knocked over a music stand during a quiet passage, making an infernal clatter at an inopportune moment. When it came time for Siegmund to pull the sword from the tree, the person on the follow-spot could not find the sword with his light. What we saw in the audience was a spotlight looking for a sword — a sight of great merriment for the audience.

The spotlight finally found it. Siegmund reached to get the sword, but it would not come out. As he pulled on it with all his might the scenery began to shake and after much effort, and much too late musically, he finally pulled out the sword. The audience was howling. My former wife was no great Wagner fan in the first place and wanted to go home at the first intermission, but I prevailed that we hadn't even heard Paul Schöffler yet and I would really like to stay in spite of the catastrophic first act (which was not sung very well either, I hasten to add).

And so we stayed. After Mr. Schöffler's glorious opening lines, out came Brünnhilde and an ocean of sound greeted us the like of which we have rarely heard before or since. I grabbed my program and put it under the light near the floor to see her name, as I had forgotten it, never having heard of her. It was Birgit Nilsson. It was something phenomenal to hear this lady when one already knew what to expect, but to hear this remarkable singer for the first time, and totally unheralded, was one of the most incredible musical experiences of my life. A voice of such beauty and power, hurling those high C's effortlessly over the orchestra was unforgettable. But Nilsson and Schöffler notwithstanding, the evening was jinxed.

In the final act Wotan bans his daughter, Brünnhilde, to a rock and surrounds her with a ring of fire to protect her from being taken by any passerby. In those days this was accomplished by releasing a large quantity of steam from pipes strategically placed on and behind the stage and lighting this steam red. As the scene was approaching we suddenly saw a bright red flash and realized that THE bulb had just blown. It would be uncolored steam. As the steam was turned on, a pipe burst and the steam now began to pour out over the stage uncontrollably. At one point, we saw Mr. Schöffler standing on the rock, waving the steam frantically with his hands trying to see Mr. Solti in the pit; he could barely hear the orchestra, as he told us later, because the noise of the steam on stage was so overpowering that it obliterated the music. It was a tarnished golden age.

During my second season, among the roles I was assigned to sing was Count Ceprano in *RIGOLETTO*. The title role was sung by Tito Gobbi, and the rehearsals were a wonderful lesson for all of us in what this art form can be at its best. I was backstage during the opening of the third act before we went on stage and noticed that Gobbi was quite nervous. I asked him about it and he admitted that indeed he was very tense. "How often had you sung the role?" I inquired. "This one is number 354. One performance was good." It gave an insight into just why this man was a giant among the great artists.

Like all Italian singers of this period, he was trained to perform all his roles with a prompter — the man who essentially serves as the conductor for the singers in many Italian opera houses. During the 1954 season, a last-minute rehearsal of the second act of *LA TRAVIATA* was called for Callas and Gobbi. Since I had the privilege to attend any and all rehearsals, I went to watch, even though my character, Dr. Grenvil, does not appear during the second act. The company had neglected to call a prompter for this impromptu rehearsal and the rehearsal was cancelled as they simply could not function properly without one.

For those of us who were trained without prompters, this was quite a revelation. These were not some dumb opera singers, but the greatest ones in the world at that time. Because of their method of training, they simply could not rehearse, let alone perform, something that they knew intimately without the help of a prompter.

A few years later during a performance of *UN BALLO IN MASCHERA*, the fourth act began in Renato's study and those of us backstage awaiting our entrances were amazed to hear Tito Gobbi making several musical mistakes at the beginning of the act. At the first opportunity he rushed offstage, asking frantically "Dov'è il suggeritore?" — "Where is the prompter?" It seems the prompter was in the washroom when they called that the act will begin. He did not hear the call, no one checked if he was in his place and the act began without the prompter, with the ensuing calamity. Needless to say someone ran to fetch him and he needed to climb into the prompter's box while the orchestra was playing, resulting in a strange traffic jam in the orchestra pit.

For whatever reason, no one had thought of connecting the intercom system used backstage to the washrooms. This had different ramifications in 1955 at an *AÏDA* dress rehearsal — with Tullio Serafin conducting, Renata Tebaldi in the title role, Gobbi as Amonasro, Astrid Varnay the Amneris and Doro Antonioli the Radamès and victim of the anecdote.

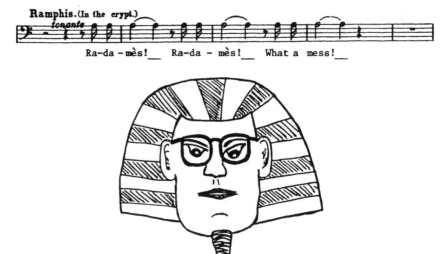

Ramphis. (In the crypt.)

Ra-da -mès!__ Ra-da - mès!__ What a mess!__

The dress reheasal was already fraught with an assortment of problems, one of which was a trumpeter on stage during the triumphal scene wearing his modern eyeglasses as he came on stage. Maestro Serafin went into a rage when he saw the trumpeter wearing the contemporary eyeglasses in ancient Egypt.

As the judgement scene proceded, Amneris sang "Radames qui verrà," ordering Radamès to be brought before her. The orchestra played the music that Verdi composed for Radamès to be brought to Amneris, but when they finished, Radamès was no place to be seen. Serafin, unhesitatingly, had the orchestra repeat this section as if Verdi had composed it that way, but when he finished there was still no Radamès anywhere. Suddenly, the audience heard a hysterical voice screaming backstage (forgive the language, but it is a direct quote) "Where is the goddamn son-of-a-bitch?" It seems that Mr. Antonioli was answering nature's call during the intermission and did not hear the call that the last act was to begin. The dress rehearsal had to be stopped until he was summoned from his temporary quarters to answer Amneris's command and be judged not only for betraying his homeland.

By 1957, the company was in its fourth season, but the array of unforeseen accidents had not abated. A production of *MIGNON* was scheduled, once again with an illustrious cast: Giulietta Simionato in the title role, Leopold Simoneau as Wilhelm Meister, the young Anna Moffo as Philine, and my old pal, Bill Wilderman, as Lothario. I was cast in the secondary bass part of Giarno. The conductor was Gianandrea Gavazzeni.

Not too long before rehearsals were to begin (and the period of rehearsals in those days was seldom long), Leopold Simoneau was forced to cancel due to illness. Carol Fox engaged Alvinio Misciano to replace him with the mutual understanding that he would be able to arrive only in time for the dress rehearsal. We were greeted by unexpected news upon his arrival. He only knew the role in Italian and we were performing the opera in French.

The bilingual dress rehearsal began, but already in the opening act, Simionato opted to switch to Italian in scenes with him to avoid the bilingual nonsense. The prompter, who himself was Italian, but was prepared to prompt in French, began to be most uncomfortable, but the act did come to an end, albeit not without some snags.

In the second act there is a quartet for Mignon, Wilhelm, Laertes (sung by Mariano Caruso) and Frederick (sung by the American Rosalind Nadell). Suddenly only Miss Nadell was singing in French, everyone else was singing Italian. The prompter began to scream, the rehearsal had to be stopped and he had to be pulled out bodily from the prompter's box in a state of nervous collapse. He was screaming that he couldn't go on this way any more, having no idea whom to prompt in what language. A doctor had to be summoned who gave the prompter a sedative. After a delay that must have lasted close to two hours, the rehearsal resumed, ending some six hours after its beginning.

The bilingual performance took place and Robert Marsh's review in the Chicago Sun-Times the next day mentioned that it was a good thing that I did not sing Giarno in Hungarian.

It was in the same season that Georg Solti, in his second year with the company, conducted *UN BALLO IN MASCHERA* with Jussi Björling as Riccardo, Anita Cerquetti as Amelia, Aldo Protti as Renato and Sylvia Stahlman as Oscar. Claramae Turner was the Ulrica, Bill Wilderman and I were the conspirators.

The opera was done in five acts. The fourth act takes place in the chambers of Renato. He is furious with his wife for what he incorrectly believes is her infidelity. After singing the aria, "Eri tu," Renato is first joined by the conspirators to plan the assassination of Riccardo, and shortly thereafter by his returning wife, who had been sent for to bid good-bye to her son. Mme. Cerquetti was a statuesque woman and her costume unfortunately accented her sizeable bosom. Upon her re-entrance she stood stage right in perfect profile. Aldo Protti, who was a rather short man, was stage left, carrying on in jealous fury and began crossing to her as he finished singing "che il cielo t'ha scorta." He really wasn't watching where he was going and as he arrived stage right, for all intensive visual purposes he was decapitated by her breasts as his head vanished inadvertently between them.

There was such riotous laughter everywhere, in the audience, in the orchestra pit, and on stage, that it was a miracle that the music could continue and the act could come to an end. Tears of laughter were running down Solti's face. Bill and I just turned our back and shook with laughter, unable to sing another note, the ensuing quartet becoming a duet for the two principals. When Sylvia Stahlman entered the stage, unaware of what had just happened, in between her sung phrases she would get near us and whisper in English, "What's going on? Why aren't you singing?" as the laughter of the audience would not subside for many minutes after this unexpected encounter. I am not sure if either Protti or Cerquetti were ever aware of exactly what had transpired to provoke this uncontrolled merriment. It really had to be seen to be believed.

It was also in the same season that Eileen Farrell came to sing the title role of *LA GIOCONDA*. She arrived relatively late in the rehearsal period, which resulted in the stage director, Aldo Mirabella Vasallo, deciding to join her on stage during the dress rehearsal, an open rehearsal with an audience of 3,500 people. He walked alongside of her, pushing her around to show her where she needed to be. As you can imagine, this was terribly annoying to her, especially as he started to push her around just as she was to sing her pianissimo high B flat in "Enzo adorato. Ah! come t'amo." That did it. She stopped the rehearsal and yelled to Carol Fox in the audience that if this so and so touches her again she will kick him so hard in a certain part of the anatomy that he will fly across the orchestra pit into the audience. Eileen was a very earthy woman, calling a spade a spade, thus I circumscribe her language of the occasion. Most of us involved in the production thought she was absolutely right, I hasten to add, both by what she said and how she said it.

Eleanor Steber graced the Lyric stage in many seasons. She sang the title role in *TOSCA* both in 1954 and 1956. In each of those productions I sang Sciarrone, and each time something else befell us during one of the performances. As Cavaradossi is dragged offstage by Scarpia's henchmen in the second act (DiStefano and Gobbi in 1954), I was to wrestle her down on the couch and once being certain that she cannot follow them, leave the stage myself. On opening night, as we arrived at the wrestling scene, her rather tight costume gave way and suddenly her left breast emerged. I was embarrassed and began to beat a hasty retreat, well before my anticipated exit as she tucked things back in as if nothing had happened. I assume by our respective positions, she facing downstage and me virtually directly in front of her facing upstage, that the audience did not witness the mishap.

It was in 1957, in the same production, that I arrived on stage in the last act just as she was set to jump off the parapet of Castel Sant' Angelo. As everyone arriving on stage is trying to locate her, Sciarrone sings, "È lei" (the sense of the text being: "There she is") and Tosca, committing suicide, jumps off the parapet. There were a lot of mattresses for her to jump on to prevent any injury. In fact so many, that on this occasion we saw her derrière re-emerge as she bounced back up.

During the previous season, in 1956, Eleanor had been ailing and had to miss many rehearsals. Thus we did all the LA TRAVIATA rehearsals without her until we arrived at the dress rehearsal. As usual, I was Dr. Grenvil and was standing next to her when she is supposed to faint. The stage direction was for me to catch her as she is about to fall. I was not well braced, and as she fell onto my left arm, we both fell flat on our rears. She laughed, turned to me as we were scrambling to get up and said, "That's OK, honey, I'll be careful at the performance," and we proceeded as if nothing had happened.

ANIMALS

I left the Lyric for the 1960 season to sing with the San Francisco opera for the next two seasons. (I subsequently returned to San Francisco for two more seasons in 1964, when already living in Europe.) I did not go back to the Chicago company until the 1974 season when Carol Fox had invited me to sing Sancho Panza in Massenet's *DON QUICHOTTE* with Nicolai Ghiaurov in the title role.

Not even the misadventures of those early years prepared me for the collection of events which were to hound this production. The stage director was the great singer, marvellous human being, and a very dear friend, Italo Tajo. The conductor was Jean Fournet, the Dulciné, Viorica Cortez.

In the opening scene it was planned that Don Quichotte and Sancho make their entrances on a horse and donkey, respectively. Oh, what havoc can take place on a stage when there are live animals. We only had the animals for the final rehearsal— a dress rehearsal that took place with closed doors, no audience present.

At the performance, as we entered the stage, the horse on which Ghiaurov was riding became very nervous as it sensed this huge audience (or at least that is what we were told), reared violently and threw him. Luckily he landed on his feet, the horse did not go through the scrim (which is what we had feared), the trainer who was with us on stage at all performances led the horse off the stage and we continued, although a bit shaken by a possible serious accident.

At the next performance it was my turn. In the second scene of the opera, the famous "windmill scene" of *DON QUICHOTTE* takes place. After the unsuccessful fight the knight has with the windmills, it was arranged that a dummy Don Quichotte will be placed on a windmill offstage before that particular

Don Quichotte with Andrew Foldi (Sancho Panza) and Nicolai Ghiaurov (Don Quichotte). Courtesy Lyric Opera of Chicago. Photo by David H. Fishman.

Don Quichotte with Andrew Foldi (Sancho Panza)
and Colleague.

blade becomes visible to the audience. As this was happening, I was to drag my donkey across the stage from stage right, where I entered and cross to the windmill on stage left where my wounded master was impaled on the blade. As I reached center stage, the donkey decided that he had enough and would not budge another inch. I tried to pull him, prod him, poke him, but he would not move.

Meanwhile, the music continued. I was singing my cues and wondered what I could possibly do with my stubborn animal. The audience was obviously having a ball, assuming that this impromptu scene was in fact part of the staging plan.

Finally I left the donkey on the stage, went to get the dummy Don Quichotte, going far enough offstage that the audience saw as little of him as possible, dragged him back across the stage, but on the floor, not draped over my recalcitrant donkey, shook my fist at the animal which was still standing there unwilling to move as the curtain came down much to everyone's merriment. Well, not everyone's. Carol Fox was very angry and assumed that this happened because the animal sensed I did not like him.

It was now time for the third performance and the first two scenes transpired without any mishap with the beasts, lulling us into a false sense of security. The third scene of the opera takes place in a dark forest and is usually done immediately after the "windmill scene" without intermission, with just a brief break to change the set.

The staging plan was for Don Quichotte to be standing next to his horse, stage right, the donkey tied down to a tree-stump stage left and for me, the trusty servant Sancho, to be lying on the ground sleeping near my master. The horse was brought on stage, we were almost ready to start when the horse had to urinate. The stage was flooded and I had no place to lie down. I improvised the scene sleeping standing up, as far from this foul-smelling location as possible, but the drama of the scene wound up leaving a lot to be desired by our own discomfort.

The next performance was a student matinee. Wouldn't you know it! Today these student performances usually occur after the run of the production with a different and a good deal less expensive cast. In those days the student matinee was part of the run of performances with the regular cast. The trainers of the animals were concerned that the accident of the previous performance should be prevented and in their infinite wisdom, sometime during the earlier part of the show, they tranquilized the horse. This had a very unfortunate effect. Just as the curtain was to rise for the forest scene, the horse got an erection. Backstage there was pandemonium as no one knew what to do.

Ghiaurov was terribly upset and started yelling to me, "Foldi, fai qualche cosa!"— "Foldi, do something!" I was yelling back that taking care of the horse's sexual problems is neither in my contract to the Lyric nor in my contract as Sancho Panza with Don Quichotte. Time was running short and management decided that we could no longer wait, hoping that this would just go away. The curtain went up. Initially the stage was dark and there was the horse standing in profile with his problem. As the lights were becoming brighter the children began to see what was on that stage and before long we saw 3,500 fingers pointing at the amorous horse. There was total bedlam in the auditorium. We could not hear the orchestra for the noise and sort of guessed what and when we had to sing. Massenet must have been rolling in his grave; then again he might have found it funny; who knows?

The horse and donkey episode of the Chicago DON QUICHOTTE leads me to experiences with other animals on stage. Starting with the summer of 1964, I spent numerous summers at the Cincinnati Opera, which in my earlier years with the company still took place within the confines of the Cincinnati Zoo. There was a large canvas-covered "theater" cordoned off for performances. Irrespective of weather, we performed. We were literally surrounded by animals and their unexpected participation in rehearsals or performances led to a great deal of merriment.

In my first season I attended a performance of *LA BOHÈME*, my initial encounter with performing in the zoo. In the opening act, while Rodolfo is writing at his table, a knock is heard; he sings "Chi è là?" ("Who's there?") and the response is Mimi's voice, which the audience hears for the first time in the opera. On this occasion, before she had a chance to answer, a parrot answered much to everyone's amusement, altering the plot for the moment. Even Puccini might have been amused by Mimi turning into a parrot in the opera.

Some years later during a performance of *LA TRAVIATA*, a camel, or some such exotic and very noisy animal, was giving birth during the evening. The poor animal seemed to be especially allergic to the soprano voice, because virtually every time Violetta was singing we heard the loud groans of the animal in labor. Freud might have loved this.

Then there was *IL TROVATORE* one summer with Richard Tucker as Manrico. In the second scene of the opera, shortly after Azucena's famous aria, "Stride la vampa," there is a scene between her and Manrico, who believes he is her son. After she has told him that his grandmother was burned at the stake, as they believed her to be a witch, Manrico exclaims: "Ahi! sciagurata!" (The poor wretch!) This is followed by a long measure of total silence before she continues to describe the dreadful scene in detail. But on this occasion the silence was broken by a barking seal that totally destroyed the mood. Some in the audience thought it funny, but this time the performers were not amused.

The timing of animals never ceases to amaze me. It was also at Cincinnati one summer that Bellini's *IL PIRATA* was performed with Monserrat Caballé as Imogene, her real-life husband, Bernabé Martí, as Gualtiero, her erstwhile lover in the plot and Julian Patrick as Ernesto, the Duke, her on-stage husband. Madame Caballé had hurt her leg sometime previously so she performed the entire opera on crutches, a condition that did not add to the believability of an already tenuous plot. At the end of her aria in Act II, Scene 2, she is on stage with Mr. Martí. Just before she was to utter her next line, "Ma qual rumore." ("But what noise."), a peacock let out some terrible sound. The end of that particular speech was, "Ah, fuggi, è il duca." ("But flee, it's the duke.") The implication was, of course, that this loud, ugly cawing of the peacock was a sound that was emanating from her husband. She just broke up and started laughing uncontrollably, bringing the performance to a temporary stop as Anton Guadagno, the conductor, and the entire audience burst into gales of laughter.

The Cincinnati Opera existed for many years prior to my first engagement there and, especially in its early days, many of the famous stars of the Metropolitan Opera used to sing there during the summer. For purposes of this story it is necessary to know that the performing stage was directly in front of the duck pond. Legend has it that at a performance of *FAUST*, after Norman Cordon, the American basso, had finished singing Mephisto's serenade which ends with measured laughter, first on a high G, then an octave lower, finally on a low G (four even eighth notes going "ha, ha, ha, ha," each time)— he was echoed after by a duck, in the correct rhythm, going, "Quack, quack, quack, quack." *[See drawing, next page.]*

Ironically, the most bizarre of these animal stories I have experienced was not in the Cincinnati Zoo, but at the Metropolitan Opera. This event has been chronicled already elsewhere to the best of my knowledge.

In the opening act of Richard Strauss's *DER ROSENKAVALIER*, the Marschallin has her usual morning "Levée" which in this sense might best be translated as a "reception." Among the hordes of people who are coming to see her (cooks, notary, hairdresser, and Italian singer to entertain, etc.) is an animal vendor. For reasons unknown to me, on this particular evening it was decided to have the animal vendor enter with two dogs, one male, one female. As he put them down on the stage floor, they proceeded to the left of the prompter's box and immediately began to mate.

We were in the sixth or seventh row in the orchestra and saw that Karl Böhm, who was conducting, had to stop because he was laughing so hard. What was even more amusing is that the singers on stage didn't immediately realize what was happening, as most of them were in positions where they could not see the animals copulating. As the singers began to inch to one side or another or trying to get further front to see what was happening, they "lost it" one by one and it took many pages of music before order could be restored.

The audience, needless to say, was roaring with laughter and one has to concede that *DER ROSENKAVALIER* is the ideal opera for such an impromptu mishap. One can only assume that management was wise enough to refrain from having dogs in heat brought on stage in the future performances.

It happened in San Francisco, I believe in 1960, when I was singing the part of the Indian in Puccini's *LA FANCIULLA DEL WEST* — "The Girl of the Golden West," in its English title. This is an opera, as my experience has demonstrated, that is somehow an opera waiting for an accident to happen. What I did not foresee is how an animal in this opera could create havoc.

As in the Chicago *DON QUICHOTTE* many years later, the horse relieved his bladder one night. I was to sit on stage for the entire third act in this production and finding a dry spot as well as trying to be as far as possible from the stench that permeated the stage became the primary job of the evening.

In one of my earliest professional appearances I sang one of the miners in a production in Chicago. One of the tenors and I were to drag on the hero of the opera in the last act, on this particular occasion, the famous tenor, Mario del Monaco. As we were running down the ramp, center stage, I uttered my first "ad lib" on stage— this one quietly to del Monaco so that he should watch his step— "Il cavallo e cacato." ("The horse had a bowel movement."— the Italian being a bit less delicate). He was grateful for the warning.

CHILDREN

At the second performance of the above-mentioned *CARMEN*, which was a Saturday matinee, my former wife brought our four-year old son, David, to hear his father. They came back after the second act, when Zuniga has finished his role and I asked him how he liked it, expecting some delight in his response. He minced no words: "Dad, if I would get up on a stage and sword-fight before all those people in the audience, I would first learn how!" Who needs a cold shower after a performance?

It was the same young man, shortly before he became three years old, who came into the living room one day with his huge stuffed dog when I was practicing and asked in a gentle voice: "Daddy, could you please shut up? Doggie has a headache!"

Less gentle was the activity a few weeks before this episode. I was making my debut with the Chicago Symphony Orchestra singing Stravinsky's *LES NOCES* with Rafael Kubelik conducting. There was much strife and excitement at home, which culminated in David hitting his very little sister, Nancy, on the head with a wooden hammer. No harm was done in the long run, but after the bedlam at home, Stravinsky was a piece of cake. Not necessarily an orthodox way to cure the nerves.

Nancy, at age five, is the subject of the next children's story. I was assigned to sing the Captain in *MANON LESCAUT* at the Lyric in 1957, in a cast including Jussi Björling, Renata Tebaldi and Cornell MacNeil. Tullio Serafin was conducting. I was preparing myself in the afternoon for the evening's performance and was vocalizing in the living room, the scene of "doggie's headache." I felt I was in very poor voice and decided to go to the kitchen to get a glass of water. We had a long corridor in our apartment at that time and I was walking past the room where David and Nancy were playing with the door closed when I overheard her telling her brother, "Boy, am I glad I don't have to pay to hear daddy sing tonight." That did not help my nerves. That night, after Björling's impassioned plea to me as I responded to him to permit them to go to America, my legs were jelly as I heard my daughter's voice in the back of my head offering her critical observation.

It was the same group of critics who observed, after I was warming up for over ten minutes for a performance at Santa Fe in 1959; "Dad, you finally hit a good one."

I was to sing the role of Baron Ochs in *DER ROSENKAVALIER* for the first time in my life in 1961 in Santa Fe. Since the children came to several rehearsals, I felt I should explain the plot of the opera, which, with all the sexual activity and innuendo, is not exactly simple. Nancy and I were doing the dishes one night when she was quizzing me about the escapades of the third act where Ochs tries to seduce the maid Mariandel, who is really Octavian, a seventeen-year old boy, in disguise, played by a woman.

Even by operatic standards, this is not the simplest of plots for a father to explain to his nine-year old daughter. When she posed the legitimate question, "What does seduction feel like?" I was not ready for a birds and bees discussion and said something like, "I can't explain it any more than what strawberries taste like. When you are older, you will find out." At this moment I heard the voice of David, aged eleven, in the living room: "Why do you bother with Dad. Ask Mom and get the woman's point of view."

DIMITRI MITROPOULOS

It was in the production of *LA FANCIULLA DEL WEST* in Chicago in 1956 that I had the privilege to encounter Dimitri Mitropoulos, the legendary conductor with a photographic memory, the like of which I have never encountered before or since. He conducted all rehearsals from memory — not as a stunt, but because he had the score firmly etched in his head.

It is one thing to hear about such a phenomenon. It is something else to experience it first hand. He would arrive, close his eyes and then say let's begin at rehearsal number whatever. The dress rehearsal was fraught with a large assortment of problems. In 1956, there were no closed-circuit television monitors backstage that enabled all backstage activity to be easily coordinated with the conductor.

The assistant conductor would cut a tiny hole in the scenery, peek through that hole to see the conductor and lead the off-stage music by coordinating his beat with the conductor in the pit. On this occasion, he was not able to arrange this in a manner to see the conductor well and the singer who was singing the minstrel backstage was unable to be together with Mr. Mitropoulos in the pit. Mr. Mitropoulos was not aware of the source of the problem and, thinking the fault was the singer's, called him out on the stage. "It can't be that hard to be together," he said. "Do you think I am a phenomenon? Please try harder," he continued in a very gentle voice. Somehow he did not really think that his memory was something extraordinary and assumed anyone could do what he could.

For example: later in the same rehearsal one of the instrumentalists in the orchestra came in too soon. Without ever stopping for a moment to think, Mr. Mitropoulos turned to him and said (I am inventing the numbers, since I don't remember the exact ones any more) "My dear man, you are at rehearsal number 422, I am only at 387." There was no score in front of him. He not only knew exactly where he was in terms of rehearsal numbers every moment, he knew where a totally unexpected mistake was taking place without ever stopping to assess where the next entrance of this particular instrument was. I was not the only one utterly dumbfounded by this extraordinary phenomenon.

It was at the same rehearsal that the opening of the last act was staged in a manner that we, the miners, were asleep lying on the stage and shortly after the curtain was to go up, six horses would gallop across the stage. On opening night we were lying down as we were told, we saw the curtain rising and shortly after its ascent we saw it descending again! It seemed that as soon as the horses were visible, the audience began to make all sorts of noises, disturbing the quiet music. Mr. Mitropoulos was so annoyed by the noise in the audience that he stopped the music, had management bring down the curtain and some announcement was made to ask the audience to refrain from audible comments when the horses appear. His concentration was such that he could not tolerate this type of intrusion into the music.

It was many years later that a story, corroborating his incredible memory, was told to me. As I began to cut back in my performing life, I accepted a position to become the Chairman of the Opera Department at the Cleveland Institute of Music in 1981. It was there I met the distinguished composer, Marcel Dick, who had his own Mitropoulos story.

It seems that many years before he had written to the Greek conductor to inquire if he would be interested in performing a symphony Mr. Dick had composed. Mr. Mitropoulos indicated that there might be a possibility, but he would need to see the score, of course. He would be coming to Cleveland in the near future and at that time he would be able to examine the work. As prearranged, Mr. Dick went to the airport to pick him up and during the drive back to the city Mr. Mitroupoulos was studying the full score intently.

When they arrived at the Institute, Mr. Dick asked him, "Well, what do you think?" Mr. Mitropoulos, with the score closed by now, told him that he was quite interested in the work, but he would make certain suggestions for some changes. He began to give a minute critique FROM MEMORY of a work he just looked at for the first time, with detailed suggestions like, "in such and such a measure the second trombone should be mezzo piano instead of forte. It might be wiser not to double flute and violin in this particular passage" (again with specific measure numbers). During a circa 30 minute car-ride, he memorized the entire score and began to give these analytic suggestions from memory to the composer. Mr. Dick, of course, was completely flabbergasted by this almost superhuman phenomenon.

DEBUTS

Soon after that season at the Lyric in Chicago when we encountered Mr. Mitropoulos, I auditioned for the new opera company-to-be in Santa Fe. It was my good fortune that I was accepted into this company where life had its own forms of amusement at performances already many years before the *THRENI* story with which I began this book of anecdotes.

My debut in 1957 was to be as Bartolo in *THE BARBER OF SEVILLE*. I never could imagine what happens to your breath singing at an altitude of 7,500 feet, nor did I have a clue what to do when you are singing outdoors and the temperature is dropping into the forties and you are singing against a wind of 30 miles an hour. No one can teach that in a studio!

Opening night of the *BARBER* was an event, but in some ways a rather unexpected one. I had been fitted for a costume, which on the one hand was no longer very new and on the other was decidedly too tight for my ample girth. That was the only costume available and it was let out as far as it could be.

I was singing on stage during the second act finale when Rosina entered the stage and she suddenly let out a loud "whoop" as she passed behind me. Instinctively, I put my hand behind me to discover that there was no longer a costume covering my rear end. Unbeknownst to me it had split sometime during the action when I was running around the stage.

I had been wearing a girdle-like contraption to hold in my tummy and since the costume was as tight as it was, that contraption was my underwear. There wasn't even room for jockey shorts over it. Here I am, making my debut in Santa Fe and I discover that with my costume having split, my back is stark naked. I sang the rest of the act sort of "side-saddle," always facing the audience. All motions I had to make were done with side-steps so the audience should not see the naked rear of Bartolo, much to the amusement of the rest of the cast.

There was a very long intermission before the last act as they tried to sew the costume as best as possible to enable me to perform the rest of the opera as intended.

I seem to have had a knack for having things happen at my various debuts with opera companies.

In 1965 I made my debut with the above-mentioned Cincinnati Opera in Verdi's *LA FORZA DEL DESTINO* as Fra Melitone, a cantankerous priest. There is a scene in the opera where he ladles out soup to the hungry masses who depart after being fed. The set was not especially sturdy, and as the last chorister was leaving, she accidentally knocked over the flat that was the church. It came crashing down, luckily not injuring anyone. But the scene could not continue until the church was put back up again.

It is easier in a comic role to get away with a problem of this nature than if you play some tragic character. Having little choice in the matter, I began to mutter about the miserable state of Spanish architecture in our time (by necessity in Italian, of course) while the opera came to a grinding halt. Anton Guadagno was the conductor, who was very amused as I went about this impromptu scene resurrecting the fallen church, and he did not begin the ensuing duet with Padre Guardiano until all was back in place again— a matter of a few minutes that seemed like an eternity.

Nicola Moscona played the part of my superior and had been in the wings, convulsed with laughter, as I went about muttering whatever came to my head while I was putting up the church. As he entered, tears were streaming down his face from laughter and he never sang a note during the scene. He just turned his back to the audience and I wound up singing our duet all by myself.

By then we had moved to Switzerland and I commuted in Europe to wherever the work was; at first from Mannedorf, our home near Zurich, then from Geneva, where I lived from 1966 to 1975. We had been in Geneva briefly before I received a call from my agent in Vienna that Erich Kunz had to cancel his engagement to sing Bartolo in *THE BARBER OF SEVILLE* for Austrian Television due to a heart problem and if I was free, they would like me to replace him. The production would take about six weeks to film and would be sung in German. Needless to say I jumped at the chance and learned the role, now my third language for this opera, as quickly as I could.

The management of the Staatsoper saw the film when it was shown some months later and invited me for the following season as guest to sing the role in their production. In those days it was also sung in German for the benefit of the audience. It was the production by Günter Rennert I had sung a few years earlier in San Francisco in Italian. It was indispensible that someone who had done the production sing it in Vienna. There was but one day to rehearse and the production was extremely complicated, taking place on three floors with nine rooms.

I arrived for my one day of rehearsal and made a most unpleasant discovery. The German translation I knew from the TV production the year before was NOT the same translation they used at the Staatsoper! Furthermore, there were two other guests in this performance — Karl Ridderbusch, the Basilio from Düsseldorf (who had another translation), and Karlheinz Peters, the Figaro from the Gärtnerplatz Theater in Munich (with a different translation, yet).

The Almaviva of the performance, the American tenor, William Blankenship, and the Rosina, Renate Holm, had the "normal" translation from the Staatsoper, and this meant that among the five principals, we had four different translations on that stage. That is a nightmare, because the various texts can have nothing to do with each other and in the recitatives when one character asks, let us say, "What did you have for breakfast?" the answer may be that "The grass is greener than usual today." This was to be my debut at the Vienna Staatsoper.

The inevitable happened. Before Basilio's aria, "La calunnia," Rosina and I were up on the second floor doing one of our recitatives. I had a word in my line that happened to be a cue word for Rosina in her translation in another recitative we had before my aria. When the bell rings, Pavlov's dog salivates. I said the magic word and she continued with what she normally sings when she hears that word, some 25 pages later in the music. We were now singing the wrong recitative, heading for Bartolo's aria instead of Basilio's. The prompter, an elderly lady who was not very fast on the trigger, put up her left hand to indicate that we should stop, made a gesture to indicate that she was lost and began to thumb pages furiously. She had only the text of the "regulars" in her score and not a word from the translations sung by the three guests. The harpsichordist stopped playing and we were upstairs on the second floor singing the wrong recitative a cappella.

Finally the prompter found something and yelled out a word for Rosina so loud that not only did we hear it but every member of the audience could hear it as well. With that, we got back to the right place again and the original recitative resumed. Ultimately, we did get to Basilio's aria.

When one makes a debut at the Vienna Staatsoper, one of the most important theaters of the operatic world, one is pretty nervous at best. But to make it under these conditions was an unbelievable nightmare. My legs just shook after this event and all night long instead of really singing THE BARBER OF SEVILLE, I thought we were playing "What's my line?"

The supreme irony of all this was that on that

particular evening the entire house was sold to a group of English tourists. Thus, our singing in German for the benefit of the audience was total nonsense, since most of them didn't understand a word of what we were singing in the first place!

EXPERIENCES ON THE ROAD

Vienna

The television production the year before was a very interesting experience. My colleagues were Reri Grist, as Rosina, with whom I had sung both in Santa Fe and San Francisco (in fact, I sang Osmin to her Blondchen in THE ABDUCTION FROM THE SERAGLIO in Santa Fe in her operatic debut), Eberhard Wächter as Figaro (more about him later), Oscar Czerwenka, a very funny man, as Basilio, and the great Hilde Konetzni, who was a legendary Fidelio and Marschallin in her youth, singing Berta — the same role she also sang in the Staatsoper production. Silvio Varviso conducted. The entire production was staged by Herbert Wise, who is probably best known in the United States for his fabulous TV production of the I, CLAUDIUS series with Derek Jacobi. It was a fascinating time.

One thing led to another, and as a result of this telecast I was invited to participate in the Wiener Festwochen (literally it means Vienna Festival Weeks) to sing in the world premiere of an opera by Iván Eröd, the Hungarian composer, who was a resident of Vienna in 1968. As is unfortunately often the case, a world premiere is often also a world burial. The opera, to the best of my knowledge, was never seen again.

This occasion, however, leads to my next anecdote. During the filming of the BARBER my management had gotten me a nice little apartment on the Danube for the six-week stay. As I was coming back again to Vienna for a long duration again, it was necessary to find similar lodging. As I had sung at the Staatsoper by now, it was worked out that the management at the opera would find me a place.

It was spring, there were many things happening in Vienna and frankly, the opera house had other things to worry about than my housing. When I called them a few weeks before my scheduled arrival they still had nothing for me. The day before I left Geneva there was still nothing and I was to call them when I arrived at the airport in Vienna, not exactly a thrilling prospect.

When I called, they told me that they found a room for me in the apartment of Mr. and Mrs. Alfred Jerger. His name was a legend in my family. My grandmother saw him as Mandryka in the Dresden premiere of Richard Strauss's *ARABELLA* in 1933. Still, a room is not exactly what I had in mind for six weeks and I told the lady that I really must look at it before I take it for that long a period. She got very upset with me and said that she cannot tell Mrs. Jerger that I have to look at the room for rent. I told her I will not stay in a room for six weeks without looking at it first and if she gives me the Jerger's number I would call them myself, which is what I did.

Mrs. Jerger could not have been more charming and agreed for me to look at the room for rent. The address would be too complicated, thus she suggested that I take a taxi to the Hofburg, the Imperial Palace, and we would meet "unter der Kuppel" (under the cupola). We described ourselves to each other for recognition purposes, I got in the cab and got out at the Hofburg where I met Mrs. Jerger.

Imagine my utter surprise when she took me INTO the Hofburg, the Imperial Palace. What I had not known was that the Austrian government housed illustrious retired singers (Kammersänger) in apartments IN the Imperial Palace and that the Jergers had an apartment there, next door to the Schöfflers! The room for rent was the bedroom of Crown Prince

Rudolf! The glorious furniture was covered in red velvet with gold brocade and the window of the room opened on to the magnificent Imperial Gardens. Now I did feel pretty silly, of course, and took the room with great joy. But I have a suspicion I know one cause that contributed to Crown Prince Rudolf's suicide at Mayerling — his bed was very uncomfortable.

Havana

In the early days of my career, travel was still a novelty, none more novel than a trip to Havana. I was engaged to sing Comte des Grieux in Massenet's *MANON* in December of 1957. It was my first trip out of the States since my arrival here in 1939, and it was with certain trepidation that I undertook the engagement.

The stay in Havana was fascinating; I had never seen anything quite like the total anarchy I encountered. At rehearsals, everyone was constantly yelling. It was quite amusing to find out how rehearsals and performances were to continue after breaks and/or intermissions. When one of the assistant conductors inquired from management about this, he was advised that when the last orchestra member returned from the restaurant across the street, he would be notified and then things could continue.

The performances were scheduled to begin at 9:00 P.M. I always had the habit of arriving two hours before curtain and in spite of the fact that I do not appear in the opera until the third act, I decided to get there at 7:00 o'clock. I warmed up, made up, got dressed and went down from my upstairs dressing room to watch the performance from the wings. I thought this would be interesting as the rest of the cast consisted of some wonderful singers— Victoria de los Angeles in the title role, Giuseppe Campora as my son and my own teacher, Martial Singher, in the part of Lescaut.

After milling around stage level for a while, I discovered that the 9:00 P.M. starting time was a myth. By the time they were really ready to start it was almost 10:30. By the time I made my entrance it was around 1:00 A.M. and my biggest problem was staying awake. When they were preparing the gambling scene, the stage hands managed to put the flats which were to be on the left side of the stage upside down on the right side— a bit of stage craft that totally eluded me. This meant that they had to dismantle the whole set when they discovered their error, trying to place the ones intended for the left on the right side. The intermission became interminably long, though the audience, out for a big social occasion, minded it a good deal less than the performers seemed to. It was after 3:00 A.M. when we got out of the theater, all of us totally exhausted.

John Crosby, who is the director of the Santa Fe Opera, had given me the address and phone number of his parents who were living in Havana at this time and they took me around sight-seeing between performances. We drove around the city in traffic that was completely chaotic. At a stop sign or traffic light, people would just honk wildly, step on the gas pedal and drive ahead full force, come what may. The number of fender benders we encountered in a relatively brief period was unbelievable.

When I commented about this, Mr. Crosby senior observed astutely that as far as he can discern, there are only two laws in Havana which are obeyed. One: "Do not cut down palm trees because they are pretty." Two: "Do not shoot vultures because they are the garbage disposal system." Otherwise, anything goes. He wasn't kidding.

The night after the opening performance there was a big dinner arranged at the home of one of the wealthy backers of the opera. After passing dilapidated hovels without electricity or running water, we arrived at a mansion. As we entered the huge marble staircase we were ushered into a very elegant living room. We were told that the painting over one fireplace was a Goya, the one over the other fireplace a Velazquez. Although I cannot possibly vouch for the authenticity of the claim, it was in keeping with the atmosphere.

When it was time for dinner, we were ushered out into the kitchen. The workers, and we the performers were workers, were not permitted to eat in the same room as members of the society who supported the opera. Without having a notion of what was going on in that country at that time, one could smell that something drastic would happen here. Sure enough, three weeks later Castro took over. Upon my return home, some of my less charitable friends commented to me that "you went to sing in Havana and the government fell!"

Milan

After a successful audition for Milan's La Scala, I was engaged to sing the part of the Gold Merchant in their 1964 production of Hindemith's *CARDILLAC*. This was also an opera in which I do not appear in the first act. At the dress rehearsal I decided to go backstge to watch Nino Sanzogno, the conductor of the production, on the backstage TV monitor. I was quite amazed to see a large group of stage-hands gathered around the monitor. I could not imagine why they would want to be watching the conductor in the pit. They weren't. On these TV sets one could switch channels and they were watching a soccer game between Inter Milan and Real Madrid. Being a soccer fanatic since my childhood in Budapest, I joined them, leaving the watching of the conductor until the second act on stage.

Naples

A few years later I was engaged to sing Alberich in a production of *DAS RHEINGOLD* in Naples. At this point I had not sung often in Italy and was not familiar with the country's labor problems and the eternal threat of strikes at the last minute. One day, we were rehearsing quite late at an hour when it was already dark outside for several hours. In the middle of the rehearsal a member of the stage workers' union came onto the stage and announced: "Sciopero" ("Strike").

With that announcement, the lights were turned off, leaving the entire cast in total darkness on stage. Trying to remember in the dark how one gets out of there, we began an exodus onto the street, fumbling our way in corridors that were pitch black, bumping into walls, corners, tripping, falling, swearing in every language the large cast spoke, before we finally emerged from Teatro San Carlo, Naples's famed opera house.

It was during this same trip that the Neapolitan propensity for mistakes on the restaurant bills came to our attention. My former wife and son joined me on this trip and over a span of three weeks, we ate out more than sixty meals. Having been warned to be sure always to check the bills when they are presented to me, I discovered that there were not more than four or five meals when there was not some mistake — never in OUR favor. Charges for items we did not have, overcharging for items we did eat, errors in addition, charging for a "big" pizza when we had a "small one," charging extra for "service" when that was included in the price and whatever else you can think of occurred. The food was wonderful, but the payment of the bill was always an adventure.

Lisbon

In 1966, I was engaged to sing the bass solos in Handel's *MESSIAH* in Lisbon with the Gulbenkian Foundation, their chorus and orchestra. The contract was arranged by my agent in London. There were to be two performances. The first one took place in a movie house at 6:00 P.M. When I inquired why we have such an unsual starting time, I was informed that we have to be sandwiched in between two showings of the movie *LORD JIM*. That made it completely clear.

The performance began and after the chorus finished singing (in English) "And the Glory of the Lord" several members of the audience burst out screaming, "Olé!" I was so surprised and amused by this that when I got up to start to sing, "Thus saith the Lord," I was still laughing and the first notes sounded like I had a trill on each of them.

The second performance took place in a church— an unheated church on a very cold evening. The female soloists kept their fur coats on (the soprano was the then relatively little-known Margaret Price, who sang like an angel). We men sang in our overcoats with our mufflers around our necks, and all of us wore gloves to keep our hands from freezing. The string players had a very difficult time of it because their fingers just could not respond in the terrible cold of the sanctuary.

At the end of the performance, the soloists were shepherded to the church office, where we were to be paid for our concerts on the spot. As I entered the room, I found a tiny little man with a huge briefcase from which he pulled out wads of one-pound notes with which he then proceeded to pay us. (We were paid in English pounds, because the agent who booked us for this concert was British). As he was counting the money, he looked a lot like Charlie Chaplin in *MONSIEUR VERDOUX*, while he kept blowing on his hands, thumbing the money.

Barcelona

In 1976 I was engaged for Bartolo in *THE BARBER OF SEVILLE* in Barcelona. We were performing at the Teatro Liceu, that gorgeous theater that burned to the ground a few years before this writing. The way the theater was run in those days was something out of another world. All the artists brought their own costumes, as was the custom there as well as in many French theaters and not unlike what I experienced in Havana, general chaos reigned.

My wife and I attended a performance of *GÖTTERDÄMMERUNG* while we were there for the *BARBER* rehearsals. The entire opera lasted about two and a half hours. Considering that the opening act normally takes two hours, one can imagine the butcher knife that cut the opera to shreds. The soloists sang in German. The Spanish chorus sang in Italian. I think the orchestra played in Sanskrit.

We were given a tour of the theater. Although all the boxes on the three floors of boxes seemed to look alike from the auditorium, each one had its own antechamber decorated and furnished in the style chosen by the owner of the box. Getting a box as a member of the audience was out of the question unless one was one of the owners — people waited for a family to die out so they could buy a box at the opera.

On the proscenium side, there were three floors of boxes as well. As we discovered, the antechambers of THESE boxes were, in effect, glorified bordellos. They were all equipped with large beds, mirrors all over the place (including on the ceilings), bidets, lavabos, and what have you.

As I came out to sit on stage for the final act at the opening performance prior to the rising of the curtain, I noticed an attractive young lady in the lowest box on stage right. She waved to me, I waved back and soon the curtain rose and we began the final act. Soon a gentleman entered the box and the two of them disappeared. Sometime later they came back. She was powdering her nose. He was pulling his pants back up again. Benedetto Marcello in the eighteenth century was complaining about the public's behavior at the opera. I am not sure he had this in mind as *A NIGHT AT THE OPERA*.

Atlanta

It was in the early seventies, having already sung with James Levine at the Ravinia Festival with the Chicago Symphony Orchestra (prior to his becoming music director at the Met), that he invited me to sing Dr. Bartolo in a semi-staged performance of *LE NOZZE DI FIGARO* with the Atlanta Symphony Orchestra. He had a splendid cast of principals (Eleanor Steber singing her very last Countess), and all of us, performers and audience alike, had a wonderful time.

After the performance, most of us went to a restaurant for a snack and when we finished I returned to my hotel room. It was around 1:00 A.M. and I was already in my pajamas when the phone rang. It was Jimmy. He said that he and Lynn Harrell, the noted cellist who came down from Cleveland to hear the performance, were going to go through their entire Town Hall recital now in a room under the stage where we had just performed. Maria Ewing, who was making her professional debut that night singing Cherubino in the performance, was coming over to sing a little and he asked if I would like to join them.

It sounded terrific. I got dressed again and went over to Symphony Hall. The gentlemen did indeed rehearse their entire concert (it was almost 2:00 in the morning by then). Maria and I sang some arias with Jimmy and we finished well after daybreak around 7:30 in the morning. That's when I returned to the hotel and tried to adjust my sleeping clock so I would be ready the next night for the next performance. I was convinced though that this is what keeps these people young. It was truly exhilarating.

Oklahoma City

During the period when I lived in Europe, I would come over to the States for periods of time to fulfill certain engagements. One of these was to sing Baron Ochs in Oklahoma City in a production of DER ROSENKAVALIER, in German. We were housed in a lovely hotel and much to our surprise, our fellow guests turned out to be a group of ladies having a convention for members of "Weight Watchers." As near as I could figure out, they were here for their final binge before joining the program. When I went down to the dining room for my first meal, I discovered a large group of very large ladies, amongst whom, in spite of the fact that I am quite fat, I felt like a sylph. They were having an orgy of ice-cream sundaes and the like. It was a riotous sight.

A few days later, the Opera Guild had a luncheon and fashion show, one of those functions I just hate to attend. As it was for the benefit of the opera, I felt that I had to show up, in spite of my aversion. The performers were seated at the head table, as is often the custom at such occasions and a gentleman was circulating among us introducing himself. I must confess I was never much of a fashion buff and in those days I really didn't have a clue as to who is who in this business.

The gentleman came to me as well and introduced himself: "I am Bill Blass." I made the fatal error of asking him, "and what do you do?" He was mortified. "You mean to tell me you don't know who I am?" "Do you know who I am?" I shot back at him in a rather unfriendly tone. I wish I had not said that. I felt like an idiot when I was enlightened as to who Bill Blass was, which I surely should have known; but, alas, at that time didn't.

The performance was to be conducted by the conductor of the Oklahoma City Symphony Orchestra, Guy Fraser Harrison. I no longer remember why, but he had to cancel on very short notice and his place was taken by a conductor from the University, whose name, unfortunately, I no longer remember. Not only had he never conducted *DER ROSENKAVALIER*, but he had never conducted an opera in his life. That is really not the opera on which to cut your conducting teeth.

One mishap after another occurred during the performance, (there was only one performance!) and the pièce de résistance happened during the third act. Frances Bible, who was the Octavian, and I were sitting at the table when, as Ochs, I try to get her drunk in order to seduce her. (This is the same scene about which my daughter was asking me in Santa Fe some years earlier). During this scene there is supposed to be an "off-stage" orchestra as well as the one in the pit. On this occasion, for a multitude of reasons, the "off-stage orchestra" was also playing in the pit.

They were placed on one side, with the "regular" orchestra occupying the rest of the crowded space. At one point the "off-stage group" began playing long before they were supposed to and the whole thing fell apart, with the two orchestras many measures from each other! Frances looked at me and, stifling her laughter, said to me softly under her breath when we did not have a cue: "With which side of the orchestra should we sing, the right or the left?" It mattered little, as many pages of music passed by before order was restored. It was an awful mess.

LANGUAGES

Opera in translation or in the original, can present its own peculiar hazards. The first time I was engaged to sing Baron Ochs in *DER ROSENKAVALIER*, was in Santa Fe in 1961, to be sung in the translation being specially prepared by John Gutman, one of Rudolf Bing's assistant managers at the Metropolitan Opera. Since the translation was being sent to me in segments as Mr. Gutman was completing them, I set about to learn the role as the text arrived.

There was an assortment of things I did not care for. Sometimes I found that the text was difficult to sing; sometimes I just did not like the English. Hans Busch was the stage director and I was in touch with him as well as John Crosby, sending them my text changes as the translation was arriving.

About three weeks before I was to arrive in Santa Fe, I received a phone call. Mr. Gutman insisted that he approve all changes that are made, a decision on his part that was perfectly reasonable, but one that made my heart sink because by then I had made many changes. Having no time to prepare a separate letter, Hans Busch sent my entire personal correspondence that I had sent him to Mr. Gutman. That proved to be a disaster.

Although I tried to be as objective as possible, explaining the reason for each of my suggested changes — which were indeed many — I did say about one particular excerpt I wanted to change that because "Mr. Gutman's English here sounds a bit like 'The cow has over the fence gejumpt." I was a fine one to talk, but what was done, was done. I was not present when Mr. Gutman read my correspondence, but I am told he hit the ceiling. My changes were ultimately accepted, but he was furious with me.

I was truly worried about what would happen when he arrived in Santa Fe. Sure enough, things could not have been icier when we finally met. On opening night his only comment before the performance to me was "and which one of us is getting the royalties tonight for the translation?"

It so happens he was also reviewing the performance for the British magazine, OPERA. I must say when I found that out, my heart sank. I suspect it was the only time in the history of that opera that a review did not even mention Baron Ochs! He just left me out as if I had not existed.

Many years later we met at an intermission of some performance at City Opera in Lincoln Center and he could not have been more cordial and friendly. Bygones were bygones.

During my years of working with young singers, both in Cleveland directing the opera department at the Institute of Music and in Chicago as Director of the Lyric Opera Center for American Artists, I tried to impress on them how vital it is to know the language in which they are singing. The great evil, especially in music schools, is to teach the singers an assortment of repertoire in languages the singers don't understand at all, in parrot-style. They take some courses in diction in these tongues, but when all is said and done, they might just as well be singing nonsense syllables for what they can communicate about the marriage of music and text.

To understand truly what a composer wrote in

setting a text to music, the singer must know that language to really appreciate, let alone communicate, what the composer intended. A curious by-product of the need to know the language can occur on an operatic stage when one is forced to improvise text or, worse yet, speak a text invented on the spur of the moment, especially when it is done in the language of the audience.

The example of the church falling down in *LA FORZA DEL DESTINO* at the Cincinnati Zoo was a good case in point. For that matter the Vienna debut in the *BARBER* and the ensuing mishap in the recitative would not have been survivable on stage had I not spoken German. Alas, these were not the only instances.

We were performing *LE NOZZE DI FIGARO* with the San Francisco Opera in the early sixties. After finishing the season in San Francisco, we used to go to Los Angeles for a few weeks to repeat the performances in Southern California, prior to the birth of the Los Angeles Opera Company. In those days, we used a version of the opera in which the famous sextet of the third act, the scene in which Figaro discovers that Bartolo and Marcellina are his parents, followed immediately the conclusion of the Count's aria.

Eberhard Wächter had just finished his aria when the four of us, Figaro (Geraint Evans), Marcellina (Katherine Hilgenberg), Don Curzio (Raymond Manton) and Bartolo (myself) entered the stage with the intention of having the Count preside over a trial in which we hoped to force Figaro to marry Marcellina (prior to the discovery of the fact that she is his mother).

As we entered the stage we were amazed to discover that Eberhard was not there. After Curzio announces that either Figaro must pay the money he owes Marcellina or marry her, according to the contract that was drawn up, and Marcellina in an aside expresses her delight at the prospect of marrying Figaro, Figaro exclaims "Eccelenza! m'appello." ("Excellency, [i.e. the Count] I appeal.") But there was no Count to be seen, so Geraint yelled this into the wings. As he and I were the only members of this quartet who spoke Italian, we now began to ad lib a recitative in F major that we cannot continue this trial without the Count. During all this, Ferdinand Leitner, our conductor, who was playing the harpsichord, was hanging on to that chord for dear life. Although we tried to make this as believable for the audience as possible, each line was really shouted into the wings to let the stage manager and other backstage functionaries know that we had lost our Count. The next 30 seconds were an eternity on stage, what with the two of us improvising a scene in Italian about how a trial cannot take place without a judge. Finally Eberhard re-entered much to our relief and we could proceed.

It seems he thought that his pants were so loose that he was afraid they might fall down and he exited after his aria to have someone from costumes do some quick alterations to prevent the pants from slipping, quite oblivious to the havoc he was causing by his absence. Most of the audience was quite unaware that we were improvising a scene never written by Mozart and DaPonte; but those of us on stage were perspiring heavily.

Let's skip to the mid-seventies to another performance of the same scene in the same opera at the Met. Thomas Stewart was singing Count Almaviva and had just finished singing his aria. The four of us entered and lo and behold, no Count! I couldn't believe it— an operatic déjà vu. This time I was the only one who spoke Italian but I had my ad lib ready from a decade before. As I launched into my "non possiamo fare il processo senza il Conte." ("We cannot have a trial without the Count."), Robert Schmorr, who was the judge Don Curzio, kept saying "Si" to whatever I said. I had to restrain myself seriously from breaking up laughing at him, while signaling furiously to the backstage folks that Tom had vanished.

It seems he had just done a production of the opera where they used the version in which he exits after his aria, which is followed by the Countess's "Dove sono," and in the heat of the excitement he forgot that we were doing the version with the Sextet after his aria. He was back momentarily, as he was still on his way to his dressing room when he heard us on stage. But it was lucky that at least one of us spoke the language we were singing or there might have been a very long silence.

Shortly after I arrived in Zurich in 1961 the company was doing the musical *CARNIVAL* (in German) and I was cast as Schlegel, the director of the circus. As there were very many Americans brought into the company by Dr. Herbert Graf when he took over as director, we encountered a great deal of anti-American sentiment with the personnel of the opera company. The irony was that not only did the Swiss resent us foreigners, the several Austrian members of the ensemble also detested us foreigners, quite oblivious to the fact that they were foreigners themselves in Switzerland.

In the first cast of the above-mentioned *CARNIVAL*, the part of the magician, one of my employees, was usually played by my friend, Bob Kerns. He was invited for a series of guest performances by the Vienna Staatsoper, and during his absence his role was assumed by a member of the second cast, an Austrian baritone. He really detested us Americans and he decided to make my life as difficult as possible by improvising in our dialogue scenes, forcing me, in turn, to improvise as well.

Although I speak German fluently (and in fact, spoke German before I spoke English— which he did not know) it is most uncomfortable to have to improvise dialogue night after night in the mother-tongue of the audience.

One night, in the dialogue before his big scene, our friend came on stage and wished me "Good morning! Isn't it funny," he continued, " I forgot your name, Herr Direktor." By now I had really had it with him and I barked back "My name is Schlegel and you're fired" and walked off the stage. As his employer in the show, I had the right to fire him and exercised my prerogative. They had no way to get into his big number after I walked off and the conductor, Samuel Krachmalnick, signaled to the orchestra that he was cutting the next number. Our friend was furious, of course, but he never bothered me again with any ad libs. One can imagine what happens to a performer under similar circumstances doing dialogue in a language he doesn't speak! The management fires you instead, sooner or later.

The language also played a rather unexpected part in a production of *THE BARBER OF SEVILLE* that took place with the Basel opera. In the late sixties, when we were living in Geneva, I got a phone call from a stage director in Basel with whom I had worked at the Zurich Opera. It seems they were preparing a new production of the *BARBER* in Basel, in Italian (where previously they used to perform it in German in those days for the audience's benefit), and their Bartolo came down with the flu. They were to open the production in a few days and my friend wanted to know if I could come over and do the dress rehearsal and the first two performances. I checked with the opera in Geneva to see if I would be needed for anything for the rest of the week and was given permission to leave town for these few days.

When I arrived, I was informed that their Figaro also had the flu and they could not find anyone who knew the role in Italian (they surely could not have looked very hard). Thus they engaged Wolf Völker, son of the great Wagnerian tenor, Franz Völker, who knew the role in German. Thus we embarked on a polyglot *BARBER*, this time four of the principals singing in Italian and Figaro singing in German (shades of my childhood, having been brought up in Budapest on polyglot performances in which the "regulars" sang in Hungarian and the guests in the original or their own tongue).

Our Rosina's mother tongue was German, but she was singing Italian. Almaviva was American and spoke no Italian, even though he was singing it. Basilio was Swiss and spoke everything fluently, Figaro was singing his native German and I, the Hungarian, was jumping back and forth between German and Italian by the time we finished.

The different translations in Vienna were a mere preparation for THIS zoo, singing recitatives in different languages. On opening night, after Figaro finished "Largo al factotum" in German, the scene continued with a recitative between Figaro and the Count. The Count explained to Figaro that he doesn't wish to be recognized here and he has his own reasons for this incognito appearance: "...Ne vò farmi conoscere. Per questo ho le mie gran ragioni." "Intendo, intendo..." ("I understand, I understand...") replies Figaro, the text changed to "Ich versteh'..." in the German translation. Wolf Völker, more to himself than to the audience, instead said, "Ich versteh' kein Wort" which means "I can't understand a word." Under the circumstances truer words couldn't have been uttered, as our German-speaking Figaro indeed understood not a word of what Count Almaviva just said in Italian.

The audience, already in the spirit of the humor of this bilingual show caught the true meaning of it all and began to have a wonderful time with the opera, part in Italian, part in German, understanding the guest's German a great deal better than the Italian from the rest of us.

By the time we got to the shaving scene in the last act, when Figaro and I have a long recitative, I decided on the spur of the moment to switch to

German myself. This caught Wolf Völker totally by surprise as he had no idea that I knew the role in German — and he promptly dropped two pages of recitative by mistake. The audience had a ball and we ended the performance with much merriment.

WORLD PREMIERES

One of the lots that befalls a singer who is a good musician is that one does get to sing a goodly number of contemporary works. And when the word is out in the profession, there are lots of opportunities to do world premieres. This can be a blessing in disguise. One does get a mixture of interesting and good works with some real lemons. It means spending a lot of time learning and memorizing a work that one will never perform again.

In my very first year in Zurich, I was cast as the lead in an opera by the Swiss composer Armin Schibler entitled *BLACKWOOD & CO.*, an opera about the manufacturing of double beds. It is really not a promising topic for a stage work. It was an interesting collaboration to get this work mounted, with Nello Santi conducting and Lotfi Mansouri directing. It also launched my career in Europe since it offered me a very good role and the critics from all over Europe came and were lavish in their praise.

Originally the June Festival in Zurich in 1962 was to open with *FIDELIO*, conducted by Otto Klemperer with Sena Jurinac in the title role. But this went by the boards when Mr. Klemperer called the orchestra some names at rehearsals for playing miserably. He refused to apologize and Dr. Graf announced that if the orchestra refused to play for Klemperer, he would resign.

Much to everyone's surprise, none of the parties budged, the production was cancelled and Dr. Graf's resignation was accepted and we opened the gala festival with this new opera. In spite of the opportunity it afforded me as a performer, I thought the work was dreadful. Indeed, after three more performances the following season, it died a quiet death.

Imagine my suprise when after the world premiere the review appeared in the Neue Zürcher Zeitung, written by the revered scholar and musicologist Willi Reich. He went into great detail discussing the early, middle and late Schibler as if he were discussing early, middle and late Beethoven. I found it all rather amusing.

Not many years later, I was invited to participate in the world premiere of another opera, *JACQUES LE FATALISTE*, by the Greek-French composer, Georges Aperghis. This was based on the novel of the same title by Denis Diderot. It was a very strange work. First of all, portions of it were composed in quarter-tones[1] which for most performers trained in Western music is extremely difficult. Secondly, it was decided that each character will be portrayed by two people, one actor and one singer. This caused great confusion in the audience, as no one was quite certain most of the time who was who.

I portrayed the "singing" Diderot, wandering about the stage writing my novel. The whole production began with the "acting" Diderot cooking a rabbit stew on stage. Since he was a fine chef by avocation, the aroma that pervaded the entire theater was quite marvellous. One of the big problems we encountered was that my singing colleagues had no idea how to find their pitches and soon it became evident that my perfect pitch would have to be put to good use for the benefit of the production.

1See *Quarter tones* in Glossary

It began innocently enough with this or that singer asking me for a note when I was near them, but pretty soon the stage director decided to do the staging in such a way that I should be near the person who needed a particular pitch. Thus, these passionate love scenes he invented for me with a beautiful blonde were merely for me to have the opportunity to hum a pitch in her ear while it looked like we were in some heated embrace. Pretty soon, I could no longer keep track of who needed what pitch when. That's when the staging evolved so that this whole thing took place as Diderot was writing the work and I carried a book around the entire time. Although it looked like I was writing things down, in fact I had a catalogue in front of me in which I had written down the entire production's pitch needs in the order they were necessary. This, too, became a TYMAR production. Take your money and run. As far as I know, it was never done again.

In the late sixties I was invited to participate in a world premiere in Brussels. It was an opera of about two-hours duration, written by the Belgian composer, Guy Barbier. The opera was a sort of *GULLIVER* adventure in outer space. We rehearsed and we rehearsed; there were changes made two and three times a day in the work itself; and by the time the dress rehearsal arrived, we were all somewhat confused.

The real confusion though occurred opening night. Between the dress rehearsal and the world premiere, management decided to eliminate 40 minutes of the 120-minute work. The opera we performed opening night had never been rehearsed. In spite of the presence of the King and Queen of Belgium at the opening performance, it was less than a howling success. We performed it for two weeks every night at the Cirque Royale in Brussels, after which it, too, died a well-deserved death.

I was not a participant in every world premiere experience. Sometimes I was in the audience. We were rehearsing a production of Alban Berg's *LULU* in Amsterdam at the same time the company was presenting the world premiere of Philip Glass's *SATYAGRAHA* in Rotterdam. Our rehearsal schedule was arranged in a way that would permit us all to go down to Rotterdam on a company bus to attend this much-awaited world premiere. Having finished an arduous day of *LULU* rehearsals, most of us in the cast piled into the bus to attend the great event. I am fully aware of the international success this opera has had, but I confess I have rarely hated a piece of music with such venom as this work.

The endless repetitive figures were driving me mad. The monotony of the stage which mirrored the monotony of the music was something that was not my cup of tea at all. I wanted to leave at intermission only to discover that we were prisoners of *SATYAGRAHA* at this point. Our bus driver went someplace for a leisurely refreshment and there was no way to get back home until the performance and reception were over.

I thought it was a crashing bore. I fear it left a very bad taste in my mouth for minimalism[1]. The moral of this story for me was that when you are performing a piece you don't like, at least you have something to do. But when you are in the audience, you are trapped.

[1]See *Minimalism* in Glossary

LULU

Although I am very fond of Alban Berg's *LULU*, it is not everyone's cup of tea either. In the early eighties, we were doing a production of the opera in Turin, but unlike the two other productions of the opera I performed in Italy, this was not done in Italian but in the original German. As much as I prefer a work of art in its original form, this is an opera with a musical language that is forbidding the first time an audience encounters it. Before "super-title" days I thought the audience could gain a great deal by having it performed in their language. Indeed, at the first few performances you could shoot a cannon through the auditorium when the performance ended and not hit anyone. They all had gone home long before it was over.

Imagine the surprise we encountered at the curtain call on a Sunday matinee when the auditorium was still full. There was mild, polite applause (much to our surprise no one booed), but they were all still there. It seems that the opera company had arranged the Sunday matinee subscription series for the populace primarily from out of town. They were bused in, and when it was all over, they were bused home. They also had no means of escape. They had to stick it out until the bus drivers came back at the appointed hour and picked them up. "Sunday afternoon at the opera with *LULU*." And for the benefit of an audience that only spoke Italian, in German yet!

As Donal Henahan observed in one of his *LULU* reviews in the New York Times, à propos the various revivals of the opera at the Met, I made a "mini-career" performing Schigolch in this opera. Before I called it quits, I had done seventeen productions of the opera and well over a hundred performances of the role.

My first undertaking of the role was in Zurich in 1964. It was a most interesting time. The management

Lulu, [from left to right] with Teresa Stratas (Lulu),
Andrew Foldi (Schigolch) and Kenneth Riegel (Alwa).
Courtesy of the Metropolitan Opera Company.
Photo by Winnie Klotz.

took the entire cast out of all other performances for the rehearsal period so that the conductor and director would have us full-time for the entire three-week period— a most unusual policy decision. The stage-director was Kurt Hirschfeld, who was the director of the Schauspielhaus, the leading theater of Zurich. As fate had it, it turned out to be his only operatic directing, as he died not long afterwards of cancer. His assistant for this production was the young Michael Hampe, who subsequently made an international reputation as a stage director of great talent, as well as becoming the director of the opera company in Cologne for many years. We learned a great deal from Mr. Hirschfeld, who was a probing and brilliant stage director.

As soon as I was assigned the role, I went to the Zurich public library to check out the Wedekind plays on which the opera is based. I turned in my call slip and waited for almost an hour before the librarian returned and advised me that I would have to go to the head librarian. Looking for him, I entered the wrong room where many functionairies of the library were working. The room looked as if it were a set in a Fritz Lang movie— little old men and women hunched over old-fashioned desks with quills and inkwells.

They were working like the gnomes of Alberich underground in a cave. I walked over to one of them, showed her my call slip and was greeted by a maniacal titter. The lady turned to her colleagues and laughingly said that I want to check out a PN. (I am making up the call letters, I no longer remember what they were). They all burst out laughing, some blushed, and they ushered me into the office of Herr Direktor. I waited a while and a stern, somber gentleman, wearing wire-rimmed glasses entered. I explained that I wished to check out a book and was told I must see him first. He asked for the slip, looked at it, got very angry, slammed his fist on his desk and roared that this book cannot be checked out; it must be read at the library.

Not having a clue what this was all about, I tried to explain to him that I had been cast as Schigolch in the production of the opera. I needed to study the plays and couldn't possibly do it in the hours left before the library closed today, Friday. When I asked what is the problem of my taking this home, he turned beet red and roared even louder than before: "Pornography!" I was utterly dumbfounded as I hadn't a clue why the LULU plays would be considered pornographic, even less, why I couldn't read them at home. After 15 minutes of pleading and cajoling, I finally convinced this guardian of morality to let me take the books home for the week-end.

I had a rehearsal scheduled for Monday morning and I promised I would have the books back on my way to the opera house. The opera house called me Monday morning at 9:00 to indicate that my ten o'clock rehearsal has been changed to 1:00 P.M., and, of course, I planned to stop off at the library to return the books on my way. At 10:01 the phone rang and the already familiar voice bellowed without a greeting: "Where is your pornography?" My explanation of the changed rehearsal was not greeted with kindness (I lived almost an hour's car ride from town) and I did have to go in early to return the books for their sacred safe-keeping. I never set foot in that library again.

One of the interesting by-products of this production was the opportunity to meet Helene Berg, the widow of the composer, on opening night. When I asked her during our conversation when she would give permission for the release of the third act (at this point we were still performing the two-act torso of the opera), she made it quite clear that she talks to the ghost of her husband every night and he expressly forbids the release of the last act. She was a very strange lady in many respects.

A few years later I was again engaged to perform this role, this time at the Spoleto Festival in Italy. The production was to be in Italian, conducted by Christopher Keene and directed by Roman Polanski. We were hardly used to the methods of the film director, who time and again called us to rehearsals where we sat for endless hours, without ever being called on to rehearse any of our scenes.

This created a great deal of tension and animosity, culminating in a nasty explosion between the two of us at the dress rehearsal, one of the two times I have completely lost my temper in public.* The upshot of it all was, however, that most of the staging of the final scene (still of the two-act torso) was never rehearsed and we had to improvise the ending of the opera on opening night to the best of our abilities.

When we arrived in Spoleto, we were told where they planned to house us. But after one night in the hotel where they arranged for me to stay for six weeks, I informed them that they would have to find me some other place, because that hotel was completely uninhabitable. After a number of phone calls they advised me that I and one of the tenors

---

*The only other occasion was when I was singing Simone at the San Francisco Opera in a production of GIANNI SCHICCHI. The alto who sang Zita kept standing in front of me. After she kept on doing this, in spite of my request for her to stop it, I finally whacked her with my cane, all in character, of course. She promptly stopped doing it.

could stay at the convent, each of us with a private room and bath. I was rather startled by this, since I have never considered myself as the ideal candidate to stay at a convent, but that is exactly what finally happened.

The stay actually was very pleasant, though also not without its surprises. Laundry was a problem, so I decided that the only thing I could do is to wash my clothes in the bathroom sink and hang them up on an improvised clothesline. What no one told me was that for several hours of the day the water was completely shut off. Thus one day as I was rinsing out some shirts in the tub while others were still sitting in soapy water in the sink, the water suddenly stopped. Until I found out what happened when the water stopped flowing from the tap in the middle of my rinsing, it became very late. I had to leave everything as it was since I had to be at a rehearsal. No one was around to advise me what to do with the shirts which were still soaked in soap but which could not possibly be rinsed out until the next morning!

During one of the rehearsals, Hilda Harris, who played the dual roles of the student and the maid, was discussing with me some music that I happened to have with me and that I offered for her to examine. After the rehearsal we went back to the convent, and unthinkingly, I invited her up to my room to show her the music. I caused a scandal at the convent. The disapproving looks, comments and snickering that came from the nuns because a woman was coming to my room would have been worthy of a Fellini film.

Since the next anecdote occurred during the *LULU* performances in Spoleto, I will include it here, even though it does not strictly relate to *LULU*. We had several days off between performances during the run and I decided to go to Rome for my first visit to the eternal city. Martina Arroyo, a dear friend from many years back, was singing in *DON CARLO* and arranged for me to see the performance. I should have seen the omen of things to come when on the train trip from

Spoleto to Rome the train personnel quite unexpectedly declared "sciopero" ("strike") and the train came to a grinding halt for several hours. It was very hot, there was nothing to drink, let alone to snack. There we sat, in what seemed like the Italian desert, for four hours before the personnel decided to resume work and we arrived in Rome very thirsty, dead tired and primarily ready for a bath, dinner and bed without even trying to attempt any sight-seeing.

I checked in at the Hotel Bologna, where I had made reservations, was shown to a lovely room and upon unpacking and undressing decided to begin the evening with a much-needed bath. I turned on the water, got in the tub but it just would not fill up. I checked to make sure the drain was properly closed and finally got out to see what was wrong. As I stepped out, I found myself standing up to my ankles in water — the pipe had been disconnected for some reason and the plumber responsible for it neglected to notify anyone at the hotel that the tub was now out of commission!

After numerous phone calls to the desk, my blood pressure rapidly rising, we finally agreed to have me transferred to another room. The hotel personnel promised they would take my clothes, which I had already unpacked and put away, to the new room while I went out for dinner. By the time I returned all was indeed attended to, but by now it was about six hours later than anticipated.

The next night was the *DON CARLO* performance. Thomas Schippers conducted a cast which included, in addition to Martina, Grace Bumbry, Gianfranco Cecchele, Angelo Romero and Cesare Siepi. It began magnificently. By a strange coincidence I discovered that I was sitting behind Gian Carlo Menotti, who was my boss, strictly speaking, at Spoleto. After the Auto da Fè scene he went backstage during intermission and was shaking his head, obviously most disturbed, when he returned to his seat. In minutes we found out why. Someone from management came in front of the curtain to announce that the orchestra and chorus are going on strike NOW(!!) and the performance will not continue until the issues are resolved.

As the audience became restless it began to make a lot of noise, which at first turned into booing and then some violent shouting back and forth between various factions (including the claque[1]) and it soon turned into a riotous bedlam. Finally some other representative of management came in front of the curtain and said the strike is because of the foreigners in the cast, which in fact was not the case at all apparently.

At this point Menotti got up in great haste and ran backstage again and after another half hour or so came the announcement that the matter has been resolved (he was apparently instrumental in resolving the problems) and the performance proceeded with King Philip's study around 1:30 A.M.

It all ended at almost 3:00 A.M. and Martina, who had originally invited me over to her place after the performance for a snack, served breakfast instead. All that was missing that evening was the Marx brothers in *A NIGHT AT THE OPERA*. To this day, I wonder at times just what keeps that country from sinking into the Adriatic now and then. They are a warm, friendly, generous people, at times leading a type of life that is utter chaos.

With this Italian episode ended, I now return to continue the *LULU* stories. *LULU* is an opera composed on a very strict dodecaphonic[2] principle. As difficult as the opera is, once the performer has grasped the musical construction of the tone rows, it all begins to

1See *Claque* in Glossary
2 See *Serialism* in Glossary

make a great deal of musical sense and, in the long run, is a lot easier to learn than *WOZZECK*, which is not based on twelve-tone rows.

The first time we were to perform the complete three-act version in the United States was in Santa Fe during the summer of 1980. After we were given the music for the third act, we all began the serious study and preparation for the American premiere. As I was preparing my part, I was quite convinced that there were two wrong notes in the score that was sent to me. The strict construction of the work made that clear. I wrote a letter to Vienna to Friedrich Cerha, the composer who supervised the preparation of the final act from Berg's manuscripts, and he confirmed my suspicions. Subsequent printings corrected the errors.

It was at the Maggio Musicale in Florence in the eighties where the stage director decided that when the opera ends (by now the complete three-act version) the entire set should be leveled flat, leaving a bare stage. The mechanical devices for his effect were non-existent, so the magic had to be accomplished by having a stage-hand behind every flat, who would then pull the flat down as the stage-hand would vanish in the dark. Not a great or practical idea.

Among the results of this idea was that the stage-hands had to be on stage for the entire final scene, hidden behind their respective flats. At best, stage-hands are not too keen about such an assignment, but for them to have to endure the musical pleasure of *LULU* proved to be a punishment too great to accept. They hated their job, they detested the opera and were not too kindly disposed toward any of us, the performers.

They talked loudly during the entire time (DURING THE PERFORMANCE), and every opportunity I would get to run off-stage, I would do so and plead with them for " silenzio, per favore" as the scene was difficult enough, without all the talking going on behind us fortissimo while we were trying to get cues from colleagues and orchestra. The only thing missing from the scene was Groucho. Ah, the glamor of it all!

One of the most thankless tasks a singer can face is to be cast as an understudy for such an opera. Understudies seldom have enough rehearsals and in a work of this musical difficulty having to "jump in" at a performance can be very nerve-wracking. The first time the opera was produced at the MET in the seventies (still the two-act torso) Carol Farley, the leading lady, was ill one night and her understudy had to go on. An unenviable task.

I had various understudies for the role during the four different seasons when the opera was done at the MET and it was, I believe, at the last revival in 1988 that my dear friend Spiro Malas was assigned the understudy task. He would have been happy to skip this assignment, as this kind of music was really not his favorite musical pastime and the last thing in the world he wanted was to have to go on and perform this role. When I arrived for the performance on opening night, I picked up the usual collection of materials at the stage door receptionist and found a brown paper bag amidst the collection of well-wishing notes and presents. In the bag was a note from Spiro and his dear wife, Marlena (whom I had also known for many years, dating to her own apprenticeship days in Santa Fe), that stated: LOTS OF LUCK, BREAK A LEG. *PLEASE* STAY HEALTHY! Next to the note was a bottle of vitamins..

LIFE OF THE UNDERSTUDY

Except for a handful of singers, most of us mortals do have to function in our careers periodically as understudies. Although this can be a big break on a rare occasion when one goes on for an ailing colleague, most of the time it isn't. You have to learn and know the role as if you were actually going to sing it. I also had my share of understudy assignments.

When I first started out with the San Francisco Opera in 1960, not only was I assigned an assortment of roles to sing during the season, but was also assigned a bunch of them to understudy. One of these assignments was to be the "cover" — as understudies are affectionately called — for Colline in *LA BOHÈME*, the role being sung by my countryman, Lorenzo Alvary.

All went well during the rehearsal period, during which the covers watched all the rehearsals but never actually got to do the roles they were understudying. As fate would have it, my former wife was arriving from Chicago on the opening night of this production and we had made arrangements for me to go to the airport to pick her up. During those seasons at the San Francisco Opera the system used for the covers was for them to check in at the stage door an hour or so before the performance was scheduled to start, see if all was well, and if the singer one was covering was in good health, the understudies were then released for the rest of the evening.

I showed up at the opera house with the intention of going to the airport right after I checked that everything was in order. But upon arriving, I was informed that Mr. Alvary was not feeling well. I was told that he would go on for the first two acts which are not especially demanding vocally and at the end of the second act he would sing through his last-act aria ("Vecchia zimarra") in his dressing room. At that time he would decide if he could sing it during the performance and I must stay in the house until then, at least, in case I had to go on for him.

By that time there was no way of notifying my wife that I may not be able to be at the airport when she arrived. The first two acts took place and indeed it was obvious to me that Mr. Alvary was not well. At the end of the second act we went up to his dressing room. I sat down on a chair in the corridor while he went to his room to sing through the aria. When I heard him, I thought this is it — he really won't be able to continue. But as soon as he finished, he stuck his head out of his room to tell me he was feeling fine and would sing the last act. I was amazed, but gave a huge sigh of relief and got out of the opera house as fast as I could before he might change his mind. I got to the airport just in time and was both amused and relieved the next day when he told me that he never sang it better. It's not what I was told by some of his colleagues, but never mind.

Two years later when I began my stint as the leading buffo of the Zurich opera, in spite of the fact that I was now a "leading" singer and singing comic roles, I was assigned some non-comic roles to cover as well. One of them was Tom in UN BALLO IN MASCHERA, which I had sung often, both in Chicago and San Francisco. The hitch was that in Zurich, they sang BALLO in German. Although Tom is hardly a leading role, he is on stage a great deal and has miles of music to sing, even though no one in the audience really knows he is around all that much.

Although I tried to get out of this, I could not and had to learn the role in German. It took a long time to commit all those words to memory, but that was part of my job. To be honest though, I did not mind that I never had to sing a single performance, even though the opera was performed more than thirty times that season.

TRAVEL ANECDOTES

One of the ironies of our profession is that a successful singer is seldom at home. One is traveling from here to there. In a German opera house, where a singer can be under contract on a yearly basis, it is possible to approach one's work almost like an "office job," spending the bulk of one's life in a relatively normal home existence. Even there the singer who doesn't get out for guest performances regularly is not viewed as a particularly successful one. In countries where this type of contract doesn't even exist, the travel is just a part of what must take place for a successful pursuit of a career.

The part of this I dreaded most was customs formalities upon entering a country. When I was a little boy, my parents took my brother and me from Budapest, where we lived, to the city of Uzhorod in Czechoslovakia to visit my uncle and his family during a Christmas vacation. When the train arrived at the Czech border, the customs officials came into our compartment, opened every suitcase my parents had carefully packed and unceremoniously dumped their contents on the floor. They then proceeded to kick everything with their filthy shoes, leaving me with a life-long terror of crossing borders.

I assume I must get nervous to this day, because I had my share of customs experiences during my travels. I can only ascribe it to the fact that I must look nervous and edgy when I see such a uniform.

After we moved to Zurich, my first engagement in the United States was to sing Baron Ochs in *DER ROSENKAVALIER* in Baltimore. With the weight limitations on luggage on trans-Atlantic flights being what they were in those days, I crammed all my stuff into a large but very light-weight suitcase, stuffed my pockets and tried to get into my carry-on luggage whatever would not fit anyplace else.

I arrived in New York, in my black coat and hat, lugging the big suitcase and was much relieved when I cleared customs. As I picked up the suitcase two men came up to me, flashed their secret service badges and one said: "Come with us please." I was terrified. I was ushered into a room where I was asked to remove my coat. After they went through all my luggage, including my carry-on, I was frisked.

"Why do you carry so much change?" "I brought back all the coins we could not convert when we moved to Zurich as I can use them on this trip." "Why did you not declare your Swiss watch?" "I got it as a going-away present from my adult education class at the University of Chicago." "Do you have a receipt for it?" "No I do not, since it was a present, but I can give you the name, address and phone number of the lady who presented it to me and you can verify it." By now I was sweating profusely. "What are these packets of sugar in your pocket?" "Well, I use saccharin, and I took the sugar they gave me on the plane to take to the friends with whom I am staying." Why I didn't leave the sugar with TWA I can't begin to explain, but I was taking it to my NY hosts where I was staying prior to going down to Baltimore. "A likely story! Jake, taste it!"

Jake opened the packet and turned to his colleague: "Hey Mac, IT IS SUGAR. Shit!" "Well sir, we are sorry to have inconvenienced you, but frankly sir, you looked bulky." "I AM BULKY!" It seems they were looking for some mafioso smuggling drugs from Naples, and seeing me in the black coat and hat and noticing that I was bulky, they assumed I was their man. What was worse, while they spent all this time on me, their man had gotten away unnoticed. I was a nervous wreck.

This engagement came to be as a result of my singing Ochs in Zurich, taking over the role for an ailing colleague. I found out that I was to appear in a very interesting cast. The distinguished Swiss soprano Elsa Cavelti, nearing the end of her career, sang the

Marschallin; Regina Sarfaty sang Octavian, Reri Grist was the Sophie and the conspirators, Annina and Valzacchi, were the young Gwyneth Jones, still singing mezzo parts before she became one of the leading Wagnerian sopranos of our time and Lotfi Mansouri, who was Dr. Herbert Graf's assistant. He was also singing buffo tenor roles to help out Dr. Graf, even though his primary function at the opera house was to be one of the leading stage directors. He, of course, is now the General Director of the San Francisco Opera.

On subsequent trips from Zurich I traveled on the TEE train to Italy. This was a wonderful first-class train where customs was more a pro-forma thing than serious scrutiny. On the whole train they would open the suitcases of only one passenger at the border. *Mine.* Always! It was quite incredible.

The first time I was invited to sing at the Staatsoper in Vienna, (the performance with all the different translations), I was not sure if they would have a bald wig for me for the shaving scene that would fit — I could not imagine that they would make one for someone who was doing a guest performance. To be on the safe side, I decided to take my own bald wig. Have you ever tried to explain to a customs official a *bald* wig in your carry-on? It is not an invigorating experience.

In 1970, my mother became very ill and had to be hospitalized for a long period. I had to remain in Geneva for the High Holidays to sing the services for the English-speaking Jewish community, whose Cantor I was. Immediately after the Sukkoth services I flew to Chicago to be with her.

Wheat branches and an esrog (a large, holy lemon might be the best description) are blessed at that service, and two well-meaning ladies of the congregation wanted me to take the esrog to Chicago for my mother. I tried to explain the difficulty of taking that, not to mention the government regulations about bringing in fruit. I assumed that was that. I got to customs in Chicago, was asked if I had any food or fruit. I told them "no," of course. They opened my carry-on (which I had not touched since leaving) and showed me the esrog! It seems those ladies somehow prevailed on my first wife, Leona, to put it in my suitcase. With all the excitement and so many important things to think about, she forgot to tell me about it. Have you ever tried to explain to a customs official that you have a holy lemon in your carry-on that will cure your mother's lymphoma and you didn't know it was in the suitcase? I was lucky that the only thing that ultimately happened is that they confiscated the fruit.

A corollary to the customs experiences is one my wife, Marta, had when we returned from Holland one year. We lived in Cleveland at the time and flew to Chicago to change planes. We had one of these wonderful customs officials who knew nothing about currency, so 1,000 Lira was the same as 1,000 Guilder to her. We were trying to explain dollar equivalencies when in the adjoining aisle they started to go through the suitcase of a lady from India.

It is well known that smuggling dope in curry is a possibility, as the presence of the drugs is much more difficult to identify when disguised by curry. It so happens Marta has a very serious allergy to curry. As soon as she smells curry, her air passages began to swell and close up and it can have dire consequences if not stopped immediately. As the curry smells began to waft over the airport, she began to have a violent coughing attack. Paramedics had to be summoned, the head of the customs department rushed over to usher her out of the area while she was trying to tell him that she was not leaving her husband alone with THAT woman, referring to the financial genius with whom we were stuck. The director finally cleared us and had us out of there, but not before Marta had one of the nastiest attacks of her curry allergy she had ever experienced.

Travel also takes a strange toll on the body when one needs to rush from one engagement to another. It happens that a conductor or stage director insists that a singer be at some 10:00 A.M. rehearsal, no matter what transpired the night before. This necessitates hopping on the first plane after a performance to get us to our destination. Or we are foolish enough to agree to do a performance that is totally impractical as far as our own timetable is concerned.

In the early sixties when we lived in Zurich, I was scheduled for a Sunday matinee performance of Meyerbeer's LE PROPHÈTE. Unfortunately, I could not leave New York until Saturday evening. In hindsight, it was a very stupid decision to agree to all this, but I wanted to do the concert in the States and by contract I had no choice but to be in Zurich for that performance. Those who have done trans-Atlantic flights know jet lag after one of those flights can be quite overpowering. I never did succeed in sleeping on airplanes and thus arrived on Sunday morning dead tired. I was afraid that the two or three hours of sleep I could get before having to go to the theater would render me useless. So I opted to go directly to the theater from the airport, resting in a seated position for a few hours before needing to vocalize and getting made up for the performance.

I played the part of one of the Anabaptists in this

opera and the three of us are on stage for a twenty-minute aria the tenor sings in the second act. The tenor on this occasion was James McCracken. According to the stage direction, the three of us were sitting on the floor as he launched into his long monologue. Once he finished we were to rise and continue to participate in the action.

Jim began his soliloquy and after about 10 minutes I fell sound asleep on the stage during the performance. Ralph Telasko, who was one of the other Anabaptists, noticing that I was dead to the world, sidled over next to me and, as an improvised part of the action, woke me up. I was paralyzed for a moment, not knowing where I was, then realized that I was in the middle of a performance on stage having fallen asleep. It took a bit of time to realize that luckily I had not missed any cues and that Jim was still singing away. It's not for nothing that my wife, Marta, has rechristened the composer Meyerbore.

Unpleasant as this experience was, a terrifying one occured also in Zurich, one that was not related to travel at all. We were doing *TOSCA*. I was singing the Sacristan and was in the wings awaiting my second entrance when a member of the chorus came up to me and said: "President Kennedy has been assassinated." No sooner did he say this than I had to go on stage. I had no idea what happened on that stage that evening. I went through my motions like an automaton, my heart and head throbbing from this horrible news. Why the chorister had to tell me this just at the moment I had to enter the stage was a mystery. I talked to Nello Santi, who conducted, after the first act and told him the terrible news. I apologized if I had made any mistakes, but there was no way my mind could be on *TOSCA* after the news of the tragedy.

Then there was the time when I was living in Geneva but had been hospitalized in Chicago with diverticulitis. I had been cast to sing Benoit and Alcindoro in *LA BOHÈME* in the Geneva production and the stage director insisted that if I was in this production, I must be at two Sunday rehearsals, because these would be the CRUCIAL rehearsals for the second act. As my release from the hospital was impending, I was able to check out on Saturday morning, take a flight to Geneva that day, go home and rest a few hours and at 4:00 that afternoon be on stage for the rehearsal, the rehearsal that I was assured was a matter of life and death. Needless to say, I was feeling pretty weak after a six-week hospitalization, but well enough to go through the motions of a rehearsal at least. I was livid with rage, however, to discover that several of my colleagues had not memorized their roles properly yet and a good deal of those rehearsals was spent trying to spoon-feed them their lines. It's a rehearsal I could have easily missed.

It was the same opera in San Francisco that was also the cause of another undesirable trans-Atlantic venture. Once again, the stage director was adamant that I must be at a rehearsal of the first act in spite of the fact that no rehearsals were being scheduled for me for an entire week after that. The night before, I was in Lucerne singing a part in a concert performance of *FROM THE HOUSE OF THE DEAD* of Leos Janacek, which Rafael Kubelik conducted with the Bavarian Radio Orchestra at the Lucerne festival.

He and his wife, the soprano Elsie Morrison, gave a lovely reception after this performance, the last of a series of performances we had done in Europe. We drove home to Zurich in the middle of the night and next morning I was off for more than three months to join the San Francisco company. I arrived just in time to be at the *LA BOHÈME* rehearsal the next morning. It must be masochism.

I had an engagement with Seiji Ozawa to sing Arnold Schönberg's *A MODERN PSALM*, first with the San Francisco Symphony in 1973, and subsequently with the Boston Symphony Orchestra. After this contract had been signed, the Washington Opera offered me a production of *THE BARBER OF SEVILLE*, the rehearsal period of which overlapped this period. The offer could only be accepted if they gave me a release for a certain number of days ṣo I could honor my signed commitment in San Francisco.

This was all agreed upon without any problems until I discovered that the stage director insisted that I be at a 10:00 A.M. rehearsal, as per this contract, on a certain date. Unfortunately that date was the morning after the concert in San Francisco. It was my error to agree to be back then. I should have requested an additional day for the travel. I had no choice. I took a red-eye flight — going directly from the War Memorial Opera House to the airport, got on the plane and flew all night to be in Washington at the appointed hour. I wasn't exactly scintillating at that rehearsal, but everyone was very understanding.

After I sat down in my seat on the airplane, a very tall, muscular, bald, African-American gentleman came on board. His looks were so striking that one could not help but notice him. After we finished our rehearsal the next day I went back to the hotel, turned on the television just in time to watch a football game. There on the screen, playing for the Baltimore Colts was the gentleman from the airplane — Otis Sistrunk. It was a weird coincidence.

Since I am discussing this engagement of *THE BARBER OF SEVILLE* in Washington, I think it is appropriate to narrate a story relating to this engagement, even though this aspect of the story has nothing to do with TRAVEL, per se, under which heading I include this anecdote.

There were to be two casts for this production — the so-called first cast performing in Italian, the second cast in English. Upon arriving in Washington for my first day of rehearsal, Ian Strasfogel, then the General Director of the company, informed me that the

"Italian" cast would perform the last act of the opera at the White House at a reception that Richard Nixon was hosting for Prime Minister Ceausescu of Romania.

Ironically, at that point we did not realize what a monster Ceausescu was (possibly Mr. Nixon didn't either), so my strong objection did not have to do with him, but with Nixon. I felt very strongly at this point about Nixon (by now, the Watergate investigation and televised hearings had been known world-wide) and I asked Ian to excuse me from this event. I did not want to perform at Nixon's White House. I suggested that the Bartolo of the English cast learn the last act in Italian, if he didn't already know it, and take my place. A day or so later, Ian informed me that my colleague couldn't possibly learn the last act in Italian in the amount of time we had, since his own rehearsals would be too time-consuming for him to undertake this task on such short notice.

Because the company had already agreed to this appearance at the White House, my refusal to perform would have meant the company having to cancel the engagement which undoubtedly would have resulted in an uproar, not to mention the danger that some of the funding for the company at that time may have been rescinded. Ian asked me, therefore, if I would reconsider my stance in order to avoid a serious embarrassment for him and the company. I realized the predicament, and agreed to participate at this affair in spite of my feelings about the whole Watergate matter.

The big day arrived and we were taken to the White House for the performance. The first thing that greeted us were the draconian regulations regarding security — surely understandable, but not without some unexpected measures. Like many singers I took a thermos of hot tea to performances, which I would drink when I felt that my throat was getting dry. What I had not expected was that security needed to check everything, including my thermos; its contents were poured out to make sure that I was not bringing any substance or device to the White House. There went the tea, literally down the drain.

The performance of this last act of the opera (which was with piano rather than orchestra) was attended by everyone who was anyone in Washington in those days. There in the front row were Nixon, Ceausescu, Kissinger and many other members of the Cabinet. At the time I agreed to perform I had decided to behave myself and not cause any problems, but I could not resist getting in a dig re: Watergate. Count Almaviva, disguised as Don Alonso, the pupil of the music teacher, has Rosina sing an aria to show how well she sings. When her aria is over, Bartolo comments that she does indeed have a beautiful voice, but that the aria she sang was boring. "In my days, music was another matter," he continues. "For example, when Cafariello sang a famous aria — but listen, Don Alonso, I will show you how this was done."

After this observation he then proceeds to sing a little ditty. In the original Italian text, this final comment began with, "Ah! Quando, per esempio, cantava Cafariello…" On the spur of the moment I decided that instead of remembering the celebrated singer's name, I would refer to the Watergate hearings and say, in Italian, that "At this point in time I do not remember his name." Those in the audience who understood Italian, like Ceausescu, didn't have any idea what I was talking about, and the ones who would have immediately recognized the reference understood no Italian. Except for Ian, who upon hearing my "ad lib" roared very loudly with laughter in the back of the room. The rest of the audience did not have a clue what he found so funny.

After the performance — and the nervous tension among us performers was enormous under the circumstances — Nixon, Ceausescu and many others came up on the stage to shake our hands. The President had something to say to each of us, and when he came to shake my hand he made some comment that it all turned out all right in spite of the problems I was causing. At first I was mortified to think that he found out about my initial objections, but it turned out he was talking about Bartolo's shenanigans, not mine.

THE ROMANCE OF THE PROFESSION

My grandparents took me to my first opera in Budapest when I was five years old and I was hooked. Little did I dream in those days that I would be fortunate enough to be on the stage one day, but I certainly loved going to the opera and to concerts. One of my very lovely early memories was a performance of Mozart's *THE ABDUCTION FROM THE SERGALIO* sometime in the early thirties. The Hungarian bass Mihály Székely, who later sang at the Metropolitan Opera in the late nineteen forties, was a national hero and institution. He had a voice of great beauty and had a low range the like of which I have still not heard again. He was the first Osmin in Mozart's opera I ever heard, and after his last act aria pandemonium broke out in the auditorium — the audience simply went wild listening to his extraordinary performance.

In addition to the vocal pyrotechnics, with a low D that actually made the walls reverberate, he was a remarkable stage personality as well. In those days encores in opera performances were permitted, and if the audience clapped loudly and long enough, an aria would be repeated. He had to sing that aria four times that night before the audience would allow the performance to continue and come to a conclusion. It was magic time for a little kid and no wonder that they named a street in his honor after he passed away in 1961.

One of the earliest concerts I ever attended, also as a young child, was a concert which was conducted by the renowned Hungarian composer, Ernst von Dohnányi (Christoph von Dohnányi's uncle), with the famous pianist Annie Fischer at the keyboard. I have no recollection any more what Mr. Dohnányi conducted in the opening half of the concert, but I recall vividly that his suspenders snapped and he spent the entire composition holding up his falling pants with one hand. Somehow I assumed that this was part of the show and was quite disappointed at my next concert to discover that losing your pants is not a normal occurence. A pity, because it was a lot of fun to watch the proceedings.

By the time I started singing at the Metropolitan Opera in New York I was in my late forties and terribly near-sighted. My initial attempts at contact lenses a few years earlier were not successful, so I opted to "play it by ear," literally. I was used to the conductor being a blur and not seeing my colleagues well on stage until we were rather close to each other. When the Met assigned the role of Beckmesser to me in Wagner's *DIE MEISTERSINGER VON NÜRNBERG*, I resolved that I really must be able to see a conductor well for a part that is as difficult as this one, especially since I would be second cast and get only minimal rehearsal.

Many months before this was to happen I returned to the occulist and decided to get myself some contact lenses and learn how to put them in. A few months before my first performance I decided to test the new lenses during a performance of one of the operas I had sung often, just to find out how I could tolerate them and to check if I could see the conductor well.

Die Meistersinger, with Andrew Foldi (Beckmesser).
Courtesy of the Metropolitan Opera Company.
Photo by Winnie Klotz.

Shortly after my aria began I got totally distracted by seeing the conductor for the first time. He was waving his baton around like he was swatting flies. I had no idea where the downbeat was except by listening to the orchestra. For the first time I also saw the prompter, whose right index finger, jutting out every time I had to sing after a musical rest, looked as if he were ready to poke me in the chest. The whole experience so unnerved me that night, that after the first act I took out the contact lenses and continued the rest of the opera relying on my ears instead of my eyes, as I had been accustomed to do. I did use the lenses for Beckmesser. Fortunately, Sixten Ehrling, who conducted, could not have had a clearer beat to follow. I really could not have done this role without seeing the conductor.

As I was approaching the end of my career, I accepted a position at the Cleveland Institute of Music, first as visiting artist and subsequently as Director of the Opera Department, the latter a full-time position. Little did I suspect that when I was going to retire from singing at first, I would suddenly get a fair number of offers to sing and to direct, which I would then have to juggle with the commitments in Cleveland. It was a lovely problem to have.

I had already been in Cleveland for my first stint as visiting artist when I was going to return to the city with the Metropolitan Opera on tour singing in the production of BILLY BUDD. I played the part of an old sailor, Dansker, and was made up to be quite dirty. Furthermore, my costume was quite weather-beaten and considering my girth, I did not exactly cut a dashing figure.

At the end of the performance we were about to enter the elevator at the Cleveland Public Auditorium when three gorgeous young ladies, who were students at the Cleveland Institute came running excitedly, calling out, "Mr. Foldi, Mr. Foldi!" I stepped back out of the elevator and turned around to see who was calling me. Just as the elevator door was closing, I heard the voice of the handsome James Morris behind me commenting to someone: "How does he do it?"

Many years earlier I was involved in a production of *DER ROSENKAVALIER* in Geneva, the only time I sang Faninal instead of Baron Ochs. The Ochs was sung by the wonderful English bass, Michael Langdon. The trio of ladies was a very handsome-looking trio indeed: Elizabeth Söderström, as the Marschallin; Anne Howells, as Octavian; and Patricia Wise, as Sophie. After a very long and tiring day we drove all of them to their hotel, and as they were getting out of the car, my former wife admonished Michael to behave himself with these three beautiful women. "Ah, do not worry my dear," he boomed. "It would be like trying to get a marshmallow into a piggy bank tonight."

TENORS

I think it was in 1956 (I am not certain of the exact year) that Dietrich Fischer-Dieskau was coming to Chicago for the first time to give a recital. Jussi Björling had not heard him in person yet, and when he discovered that we were going to the concert, asked if he could join us. I was fortunate enough to get three box seats and when we arrived at Orchestra Hall, Mr. Björling insisted that he sit in the second row behind us as he did not want to be noticed. After Fischer-Dieskau finished his first selection, Mr. Björling leaned forward and whispered in my ear: "A very talented tenor!" He would have none of his baritone billing.

In 1983 I was singing Mathieu in a production of *ANDREA CHENIER* in Miami. By then I had become a great fan of Guayabera shirts, the Mexican and/or Philipino shirts one wears over one's slacks. They can be very beautiful and when you are chubby, they do hide a multitude of sins. I went to a store to see if they had some in my size. The salesperson did not know if he could get some before I was to leave town and was going to give me a call to let me know.

One day when the phone rang, my wife, Marta, answered and hearing a Spanish accent in the caller's voice, called out to me to get the phone. She thought it's the Guayabera salesman calling. You can imagine our surprise to find out it wasn't the salesman, but the tenor singing the title role of the production, Placido Domingo. He was returning a call to let us know that he would not be able to join us for dinner that night.

THE MUSIC CRITIC

When I first went into music as my major field at the University of Chicago, it was to major in musicology. My secret hope in those days was to become a music critic. After a while I got a position on the University's newspaper, the Chicago Maroon, to be its music critic. I attended whatever concerts, opera and ballet I could, as the various music organizations of the city were hardly going to give free tickets to the University's newspaper. More often than not, I went to the opera or ballet as an usher. (In the forties the Chicago Symphony Orchestra had a much more organized system of ushers than the volunteers at the Opera House where one lined up at a door to usher and they used you on a first-come basis).

The Chicago Times, a tabloid and one of the four daily newspapers in those days, decided in January of 1947 that it did not need a music critic. Its readership, they felt, was hardly the type that cared about classical music. Thus they let their music critic go. In April they had a change of heart when they realized that the Metropolitan Opera was coming to Chicago on tour and they really ought to cover this occasion.

Subsequent events made me suspect that they may have gotten just enough complaints from their readership for no coverage of any musical events, including the weekly concerts of the Chicago Symphony Orchestra. I think they came to the conclusion that they really ought to have a music critic after all.

Things must have gotten put off or delayed at the paper, because on a certain Thursday no attempts had been made yet to get a critic by Monday when the Met arrived. Thus, on Friday morning, Robert Pollak, who was the drama critic, had been assigned to get a music critic by Monday. Among the people he called on that Friday morning to find a critic for the Times was one of my professors at the University, Siegmund

Levarie. He told Mr. Pollak that he had just the man for the job and without an interview, sight unseen, I was hired to be *THE* music critic for one of the major daily newspapers of Chicago. Friday night I was ushering in the upper balcony of the Civic Opera House for the ballet. Monday I was sitting in the fifth row on the main floor reviewing Ezio Pinza in the title role of *BORIS GODUNOV.*

It was certainly a very interesting turn of events. Here I was, a graduate student still (another year before I would have my M.A. in musicology), reviewing Chicago's musical life for the Chicago Times. The responsibility weighed heavily on my shoulders, but at the same time I suffered from the brashness of youth. I was going to set the musical world right. After all, when you are twenty-one, you think you know everything. Only later did I discover how far from the truth that is. There were several unforeseen experiences I encountered, some due to my zeal and gall, some were assortments of odd programs or occurences, but some due to my ignorance of the newspaper business.

I had no idea that one does not write one's own headlines. A critic with Claudia Cassidy's clout at the Tribune could write her own, but most of us mortals did not. This came home to haunt me one night when I was reviewing a concert played by the Chicago Women's Symphony Orchestra, conducted by Izler Solomon.

They opened their concert with the Overture to Kabalevsky's *COLAS BREUGNON.* I considered the piece rather corny, and said so in my review. The next morning I was mortified to read the headline over my review: "Women's Symphony Pops Corn." Friends and colleagues were also not aware that I had no control over the headline and I had a lot of explaining to do.

I reviewed a concert by the Jewish People's Choral Society at which the Hungarian tenor, Miklós

Gáfni. was the guest soloist. Among his selections was Canio's aria from *I PAGLIACCI*, "Vesti la giubba." The composer was identified in the program as Leon Cavallo. Good old Leon, what a splendid aria he wrote.

In the summer of 1947 I reviewed concerts both at Ravinia Park, the summer home of the Chicago Symphony Orchestra, and at Grant Park. One of a series of concerts at the latter were a set of Beethoven concerts conducted by Antal Doráti, about whom I had often heard in Budapest from my grandmother. Not only did I decide that I knew better than he, but I made my dislike for his concert obnoxious, to say the least.

I began my review of the first concert with: "Antal Doráti played Beethoven yesterday. Beethoven lost." Even if I were right, which I probably was not, it was a nasty way to write and I am very sorry in retrospect that I did that. I assumed that my readership was almost nonexistent and besides, who would read the Chicago Times for music reviews? Surely no one in the profession. Some years later when I had begun my own singing career, Mr. Doráti was in Chicago auditioning singers for Mendelssohn's *DIE ERSTE WALPURGISNACHT*, which he was going to conduct with the Dallas Symphony Orchestra, whose music director he was. I went to audition for him. After I finished, he asked me in Hungarian if I am the Foldi who used to write for the *Chicago Times*? With trepidation I responded, "Yes." He was a gentleman and all he said was, "Thank you." I did not get the job.

I was reviewing the Chicago Symphony Orchestra regularly at Orchestra Hall the next autumn. Its music director was Artur Rodzinski. Although I certainly admired him immensely, I would find this or that to carp about. I had also asked him if I could attend rehearsals, provided that the activities of the rehearsal were strictly confidential. He wrote back that he has no objection to my attending the rehearsals if incidents at the rehearsal were indeed confidential. In a handwritten PS to his letter of November 1, 1947, he took exception to two comments in the previous review. He wrote: "The repeat in the Beethoven scherzo is *traditional*. There was only *one* cut in the Tchaikovsky fifth."

Some weeks later, when I was in a music history class, someone from the music department office came in and whispered something in the professor's ear. He turned to me and said that there was a special press conference at Orchestra Hall and I must leave immediately to attend. It didn't exactly endear me to my fellow students, I confess.

I went downtown to the conference, where we were greeted with the news that the board of the Chicago Symphony had fired Artur Rodzinski. This is hardly the place to go into the causes and reasons for this drastic action. But what emerged subsequently is that, for whatever reason, Mr. Rodzinski was not informed of this and he found out at home that night at dinner, listening to the radio! Welcome to the music business.

That same autumn, Fortune Gallo's San Carlo Opera Company was coming to Chicago for a week. This was a touring company with a few very good singers, but the rest were less than first-rate. After witnessing the third performance, I wrote in my review that I thought it was a spontaneous, unrehearsed event and that the public is being taken for a ride purchasing tickets to such events. Little did I suspect the consequences of these utterances.

I arrived Thursday evening at the Opera House for that night's performance when the head usher told me, as I entered, that the gentleman who is sponsoring these performances wants to see me in his office. I went to see him and he immediately informed me that he does not like what he is reading in the *Times* about these performances. His box office is being ruined (somehow I found it quite incredible that my reviews would be responsible for the sagging box office) and if I don't stop writing this way, he will have "his boys take me for a ride."

I was panic-stricken. I sat through the performance and went to my managing editor at the paper immediately when I got to the office that night and told him what happened. He asked me what I intended to do? I told him that I cannot say in clear conscience that these performances are good because I think they are dreadful. He turned to me in great seriousness and said that he respects my integrity, but he really is concerned that the man in question might have "meant business."

He really does not want to have to write a headline about a dead music critic fished out of the Chicago river in order to sell newspapers and he had the following suggestion to make: "The *Times* is really not paying you a good salary and no one can expect you to review every musical event in the city on such a poor pay." He suggested that I stop reviewing the San Carlo performances, starting immediately. This way I will not have to compromise my standards and I will also not run the risk of being "bumped off." This was hardly what I imagined the life of a music critic to be.

In retrospect, I was lucky that during this rash of negative reviews I praised the conducting of Nicola Rescigno, who was one of the triumvirate who hired me for the Lyric Theater's initial season in 1954, and equally fortunate that I wrote well of the bass, William Wilderman, with whom I sang often in the same company.

One day in December, I went to Orchestra Hall to review a performance of *MESSIAH*. As members of the orchestra, especially brass and percussion, have long waits between numbers in which they play in this oratorio, they either follow the performance as listeners, or, as it occasionally happens, they prop up something small on their music stand, like *Reader's Digest*. They read the magazine, paying absolutely no attention to what is happening around them on stage. On this particular occasion the trumpeter was deeply engrossed in some article when he thought the aria, "The trumpet shall sound" was about to begin. He mistook the conductor's sign to someone else and let out a very loud sound on his trumpet in the middle of a quiet, ethereal passage. He was enormously embarrassed, as well he should have been, having ruined the mood of the entire performance by this gaffe. Frankly, to this day I cannot understand why on stage such behavior is condoned or permitted.

In December of 1947, I came down with pneumonia and had to be hospitalized. The concert I was to review that week had Vladimir Horowitz as soloist, hardly a concert we could not review.

One of my good friends and my successor on the Chicago Maroon was James Goldman, who subsequently won an Oscar for his script of the film, "*THE LION IN WINTER.*" Jim was a cellist, was in music school with me and was very knowledgeable. After a lengthy discussion, we hit on a solution. He would review the concert and write the article under my name. I gave him my tickets and he did just that. "Oh, you'll probably get fired for this," he joked.

The next morning when I awoke in the hospital the paper boy did not have the *Times*, but he did have the *Tribune*. I bought it and the following headline greeted my eyes: "*Sun* and *Times* to combine; many may lose jobs."

That weekend the *Chicago Sun* and *Chicago Times* combined to form the new newspaper, the *Chicago Sun-Times*. Half of the combined staff was let go. There was not much doubt who would get the job of the music critic on the newly-formed paper. The critic of the *Sun* was Felix Borowski, the dean of the Chicago critics at the time and it was a foregone conclusion that he would be given the position and I would be fired. Jim Goldman's review of the Horowitz concert was indeed the last review to appear under my byline!

STRAVINSKY AND HINDEMITH

Having begun this monograph of anecdotes with a story about Igor Stravinsky, I thought it might be appropriate to end it with some stories about him and Paul Hindemith, as well.

It was in the summer of 1961 that John Crosby invited both of these giants of twentieth century music to be at the Santa Fe Opera. Paul Hindemith conducted the performances of his opera *THE NEWS OF THE DAY*, and I played the part of Baron D'Houdoux in the production. These were the years of the original theater in Santa Fe, a theater in which the audience was sitting totally in the open, unprotected from the elements. Although the stage had a roof over it, when it rained and the wind would start blowing the rain in our direction, the orchestra pit would be emptied first, as the instruments had to be protected and soon thereafter, in most cases we would have to abandon proceedings on the stage as well.

At the second performance a tremendous rain storm occurred. Mr. Hindemith conducted with someone holding an umbrella over him. He was so rapt in what he was doing that he did not realize at first that members of the orchestra were fleeing the pit, one by one. Since we were ankle deep in water on stage, I looked down to see this amazing sight of Paul Hindemith conducting with a black umbrella over him, almost oblivious to the fact that by then no one was playing. Soon we all folded our tents.

It was during the rehearsal period of this opera that Igor Stravinsky was arriving in Santa Fe to oversee the revival of *OEDIPUS REX* from the previous summer and the new production of his *PERSÉPHONE*.

Mr. Hindemith was rehearsing us when the news spread that Mr. Stravinsky had arrived at the opera. The two apparently had never met before. Mr. Hindemith was visibly excited and the rehearsal was stopped as we all watched an auspicious page in music history, the meeting of Hindemith and Stravinsky.

IGOR STRAVINSKY'S *OEDIPUS REX*

It was during the previous summer that I participated in the *OEDIPUS* production which Mr. Stravinsky, himself, conducted. The costumes, designed by Mrs. Vera Stravinsky, were such that we wore masks which were cut in a manner so that we had to watch Mr. Stravinsky by peering out under the bottom of the half-mask. Trying to see him through the eye-holes would have positioned our heads in such a way that all of us would have been singing into the floor.

As I entered the stage, singing the role of Tiresias, it dawned on me that this was like singing in *DON GIOVANNI* with Mozart conducting. As I looked down to see Mr. Stravinsky, after my first word he stopped conducting and leaned against the back of the orchestra pit. During the entire aria he remained in this position and I assumed that he was suddenly taken ill and was obviously very much concerned about him.

After my exit into the wings I was watching him intently and he suddenly resumed conducting. As in my opening anecdote, I rushed to him after the performance to find out why he had to stop conducting during my aria. He smiled at me and said: "You are a very good musician and you don't really need me. I am an old man and needed the rest and I thought this was the best time for it."

How ironic that both times I sang under his direction he stopped conducting in the middle of a performance! This time to rest; previously to pray.

GLOSSARY

Serialism. (Simplified explanation) The discarding of traditional principles of tonality, melody, harmony and rhythm in the twelve-tone row or dodecaphonism, was adapted by Stravinsky in many of his late compositions. In this system, according to this principle, all twelve notes of the chromatic scale are to be used once before they can be repeated. Once this dodecaphonic row is established, the row is then repeated and is the basis of the entire composition. Because the absence of tonality, it is often difficult for singers to find the initial pitch of a phrase in this system, especially if the music is a cappella (unaccompanied).

Canon. A device of counterpoint whereby a melody is imitated in its entirety by one or more of the voices, each beginning a fixed number of notes later. The *round*, like "Row, row, row your boat," belongs to this genre of music.

Transposition. Rewriting or performing a composition, or part of a composition, in a different key than which it is writen — for example if a piece is written in "G" major, performing it one step lower, in "F" major. In a composition like THRENI, it would entail singing a section higher or lower than it is written, even though no "key" can be involved here. If one transposes a section a half step lower than written, for example, one sings "A-flat" when one sees an "A," a "C" when one sees a "D-flat," etc.

Monodia (Monody). Music that exists as a single melodic line.

Quarter tones. Traditional Western music divides the octave into twelve equal semitones. If each of these is divided once again, the music is based on octaves which are divided into twenty four quarter tones. The folk music of some countries is based on a system which divides the octave into smaller microtones than the semitone, though not necessarily into equal quarter tones. Music of some twentieth century composers, like this composition by Georges Aperghis, is composed on a principle of twenty-four equal quarter tones to the octave.

Minimalism. A vague term for music which employs rudimentary materials (often simple diatonic scales and triads) and repetitive rhythmic and melodic figures.

Claque. A group of audience members who are paid to applaud, boo or otherwise vocally manifest approval or disapproval.

Elixir of Love, with Andrew Foldi (Dulcamara).
Cinncinati Zoo Opera, 1968.
Courtesy of Marshall C. Hunt, Jr., Photographer

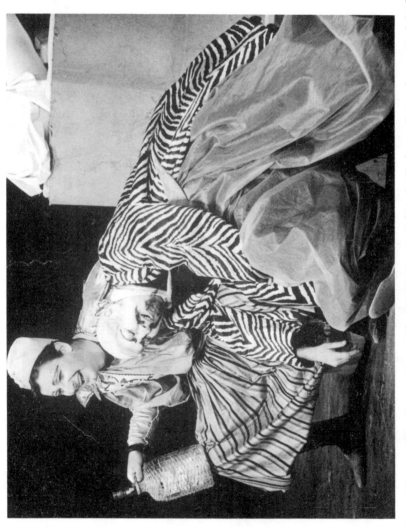

Abduction From The Seraglio with Nico Castel (Pedrillo) and Andrew Foldi (Osmin). Courtesy of The Santa Fe Opera. Photo by Tony Perry.

Anna Bolena, with Andrew Foldi (Henry VIII).
Courtesy of Santa Fe Opera, 1959.
Photo by Tony Perry.